MACMILLAN M...

HENRY V

BY WILLIAM SHAKESPEARE

PETER DAVISON

with an Introduction by
HAROLD BROOKS

MACMILLAN
EDUCATION

First edition 1987

Published by
MACMILLAN EDUCATION LTD
Houndmills, Basingstoke, Hampshire RG21 2XS
and London
Companies and representatives
throughout the world

Typeset by TecSet

Printed in Hong Kong

British Library Cataloguing in Publication Data
Davison, P. H.
Henry V by William Shakespeare.—
(Macmillan master guides)
1. Shakespeare, William. Henry V
I. Title   II. Shakespearce, William. Henry V
822.3'3   PR2812
ISBN 0–333–41671–6 Pbk
ISBN 0–333–41672–4 Pbk export

CONTENTS

GENERAL EDITOR'S PREFACE

The aim of the Macmillan Master Guides is to help you to appreciate the book you are studying by providing information about it and by suggesting ways of reading it which will lead to a fuller understanding. The section on the writer's life and background has been designed to illustrate those aspects of the writer's life which have influenced the work, and to place it in its personal and literary context. The summaries and critical commentary are of special importance in that each brief summary of the action is followed by an examination of the significant critical points. The space which might have been given to repetitive explanatory notes has been devoted to a detailed analysis of the kind of passage which might confront you in an examination. Literary criticism is concerned with both the broader aspects of the work being studied and with its detail. The ideas which meet us in reading a great work of literature, and their relevance to us today, are an essential part of our study, and our Guides look at the thought of their subject in some detail. But just as essential is the craft with which the writer has constructed his work of art, and this may be considered under several technical headings – characterisation, language, style and stagecraft, for example.

The authors of these Guides are all teachers and writers of wide experience, and they have chosen to write about books they admire and know well in the belief that they can communicate their admiration to you. But you yourself must read and know intimately the book you are studying. No one can do that for you. You should see this book as a lamp-post. Use it to shed light, not to lean against. If you know your text and know what it is saying about life, and how it says it, then you will enjoy it, and there is no better way of passing an examination in literature.

JAMES GIBSON

AN INTRODUCTION TO THE STUDY OF SHAKESPEARE'S PLAYS

A play as a work of art exists to the full only when performed. It must hold the audience's attention throughout the performance, and, unlike a novel, it can't be put down and taken up again. It is important to experience the play as if you are seeing it on the stage for the first time, and you should begin by reading it straight through. Shakespeare builds a play in dramatic units which may be divided into smaller subdivisions, or episodes, marked off by exits and entrances and lasting as long as the same actors are on the stage. Study it unit by unit.

The first unit provides the exposition which is designed to put the audience into the picture. In the second unit we see the forward movement of the play as one situation changes into another. The last unit in a tragedy or a tragical play will bring the catastrophe and in comedy — and some of the history plays — an unravelling of the complications, what is called a *dénouement*.

The onward movement of the play from start to finish is its progressive structure. We see the chain of cause and effect (the plot) and the progressive revelation and development of character. The people, their characters and their motives drive the plot forward in a series of scenes which are carefully planned to give variety of pace and excitement. We notice fast-moving and slower-moving episodes, tension mounting and slackening, and alternative fear and hope for the characters we favour. Full-stage scenes, such as stately councils and processions or turbulent mobs, contrast with scenes of small groups or even single speakers. Each of the scenes presents a deed or event which changes the situation. In performance, entrances and exits and stage actions are physical facts, with more impact than on the page. That impact Shakespeare relied upon, and we must restore it by an effort of the imagination.

Shakespeare's language is just as diverse. Quickfire dialogue is followed by long speeches, and verse changes to prose. There is a wide range of speech — formal, colloquial, dialect, 'Mummerset' and the broken English of foreigners, for example. Songs, instrumental music, and the noise of battle, revelry and tempest, all extend the range of dramatic expression. The dramatic use of language is enhanced by skilful stagecraft, by costumes, by properties such as beds, swords and Yorick's skull, by such stage business as kneeling, embracing and giving money, and by use of such features of the stage structure as the balcony and the trapdoor.

By these means Shakespeare's people are brought vividly to life and cleverly individualised. But though they have much to tell us about human nature, we must never forget that they are characters in a play, not in real life. And remember, they exist to enact the play, not the play to portray *them*.

Shakespeare groups his characters so that they form a pattern, and it is useful to draw a diagram showing this. Sometimes a linking character has dealings with each group. The pattern of persons belongs to the symmetric structure of the play, and its dramatic unity is reinforced and enriched by a pattern of resemblances and contrasts; for instance, between characters, scenes, recurrent kinds of imagery, and words. It is not enough just to notice a feature that belongs to the symmetric structure, you should ask what its relevance is to the play as a whole and to the play's ideas.

These ideas and the dramatising of them in a central theme, or several related to each other, are a principal source of the dramatic unity. In order to see what themes are present and important, look, as before, for pattern. Observe the place in it of the leading character. In tragedy this will be the protagonist, in comedy heroes and heroines, together with those in conflict or contrast with them. In *Henry IV Part I*, Prince Hal is being educated for kingship and has a correct estimate of honour, while Falstaff despises honour, and Hotspur makes an idol of it. Pick out the episodes of great intensity as, for example, in *King Lear* where the theme of spiritual blindness is objectified in the blinding of Gloucester, and similarly, note the emphases given by dramatic poetry as in Prospero's 'Our revels now are ended . . .' or unforgettable utterances such as Lear's 'Is there any cause in Nature that makes these hard hearts?' Striking stage-pictures such as that of Hamlet behind the King at prayer will point to leading themes, as will all the parallels and recurrences, including those of phrase and imagery. See whether, in the play you are studying, themes known to be favourites with Shakespeare are prominent, themes such as those of order and dis-order, relationships disrupted by mistakes about identity, and appearance and reality. The latter were bound to fascinate Shakespeare, whose theatrical art worked by means of illusions which pointed beyond the surface of actual life to underlying truths. In looking at themes beware of attempts to make the play fit some orthodoxy a critic believes in − Freudian perhaps, or Marxist, or dogmatic Christian theology − and remember that its ideas, though they often have a bearing on ours, are Elizabethan.

Some of Shakespeare's greatness lies in the good parts he wrote for the actors. In his demands upon them, and the opportunities he provided, he bore their professional skills in mind and made use of their physical prowess, relished by a public accustomed to judge fencing and wrestling as expertly as we today judge football and tennis. As a member of the professional group of players called the Chamberlain's Men he knew each actor he was writing for. To play his women he had highly trained boys. As paired heroines they were often contrasted, short with tall, for example, or one vivacious and enterprising, the other more conventionally feminine.

Richard Burbage, the company's leading man, was famous as a great tragic actor, and he took leading roles in seven of Shakespeare's tragedies. Though each of the seven has its own distinctiveness, we shall find at the centre of all of them a tragic protagonist possessing tragic greatness, not just one 'tragic flaw' but a tragic vulnerability. He will have a character which makes him unfit to cope with the tragic situations confronting him, so that his tragic errors bring down upon him tragic suffering and finally a tragic catastrophe. Normally, both the suffering and the catastrophe are far worse than he can be said to deserve, and others are engulfed in them who deserve such a fate less or not at all. Tragic terror is aroused in us because, though exceptional, he is sufficiently near to normal humankind for his fate to remind us of what can happen to human beings like ourselves, and because we see in it a combination of inexorable law and painful mystery. We recognise the principle of cause and effect where in a tragic world errors return upon those who make them, but we are also aware of the tragic disproportion between cause and effect. In a tragic world you may kick a stone and start an avalanche which will destroy you and others with you. Tragic pity is aroused in us by this disproportionate suffering, and also by all the kinds of suffering undergone by every character who has won our imaginative sympathy. Imaginative sympathy is wider than moral approval, and is felt even if suffering does seem a just and logical outcome. In addition to pity and terror we have a sense of tragic waste because catastrophe has affected so much that was great and fine. Yet we feel also a tragic exaltation. To our grief the men and women who represented those values have been destroyed, but the values themselves have been shown not to depend upon success, nor upon immunity from the worst of tragic sufferings and disaster.

Comedies have been of two main kinds, or cross-bred from the two. In critical comedies the governing aim is to bring out the absurdity or irrationality of follies and abuses, and make us laugh at them. Shakespeare's comedies often do this, but most of them belong primarily to the other kind – romantic comedy. Part of the romantic appeal is to our liking for suspense; they are dramas of averted threat, beginning in trouble and ending in joy. They appeal to the romantic senses of adventure and of wonder, and to complain that they are improbable is silly because the improbability, the marvellousness, is part of the pleasure. They dramatise stories of romantic love, accompanied by love doctrine – ideas and ideals of love. But they are plays in two tones, they are comic as well as romantic. There is often something to laugh at even in the love stories of the nobility and gentry, and just as there is high comedy in such incidents as the cross-purposes of the young Athenians in the wood, and Rosalind as 'Ganymede' teasing Orlando, there is always broad comedy for characters of lower rank. Even where one of the sub-plots has no effect on the main plot, it may take up a topic from it and present it in a more comic way.

What is there in the play to make us laugh or smile? We can distinguish many kinds of comedy it may employ. *Language* can amuse by its wit, or by absurdity, as in Bottom's malapropisms. Feste's nonsense-phrases, so fatuously admired by Sir Andrew, are deliberate, while his catechising of Olivia is clown-routine. Ass-headed Bottom embraced by the Fairy Queen is a *comic spectacle* combining costume and stage-business. His wanting to play every part is *comedy of character*. Phebe disdaining Silvius and in love with 'Ganymede', or Malvolio treating Olivia as though she had written him a love-letter is *comedy of situation*; the situation is laughably different from what Phebe or Malvolio supposes. A comic let-down or anticlimax can be devastating, as we see when Aragon, sure that he deserves Portia, chooses the silver casket only to find the portrait not of her but of a 'blinking idiot'. By *slapstick, caricature* or sheer *ridiculousness of situation*, comedy can be exaggerated into farce, which Shakespeare knows how to use on occasion. At the opposite extreme, before he averts the threat, he can carry it to the brink of tragedy, but always under control.

Dramatic irony is the result of a character or the audience anticipating an outcome which, comically or tragically, turns out very differently. Sometimes *we* foresee that it will. The speaker never foresees how ironical, looking back, the words or expectations will appear. When she says, 'A little water clears us of this deed' Lady Macbeth has no prevision of her sleep-walking words, 'Will these hands ne'er be clean?' There is irony in the way in which in all Shakespeare's tragic plays except *Richard II* comedy is found in the very heart of the tragedy. The Porter scene in *Macbeth* comes straight after Duncan's murder. In *Hamlet* and *Antony and Cleopatra* comic episodes lead into the catastrophe: the rustic Countryman brings Cleopatra the means of death, and the satirised Osric departs with Hamlet's assent to the fatal fencing match. The Porter, the Countryman and Osric are not mere 'comic relief', they contrast with the tragedy in a way that adds something to it, and affects our response.

A sense of the comic and the tragic is common ground between Shakespeare and his audience. Understandings shared with the audience are necessary to all drama. They include conventions, i.e. assumptions, contrary to what factual realism would demand, which the audience silently agrees to accept. It is, after all, by a convention, what Coleridge called a 'willing suspension of disbelief', that an actor is accepted as Hamlet. We should let a play teach us the conventions it depends on. Shakespeare's conventions allow him to take a good many liberties, and he never troubles about inconsistencies that wouldn't trouble an audience. What matters to the dramatist is the effect he creates. So long as we are responding as he would wish, Shakespeare would not care whether we could say by what means he has made us do so. But to appreciate his skill, and get a fuller understanding of his play, we have to distinguish these means, and find terms to describe them.

If you approach the Shakespeare play you are studying bearing in mind what is said to you here, then you will respond to it more fully than before. Yet like all works of artistic genius, Shakespeare's can only be analysed so far. His drama and its poetry will always have about them something 'which into words no critic can digest'.

HAROLD BROOKS

Acknowledgements

Textual references to the Commentary are by Act and Scene (e.g. IV.viii); those to the rest of the text are by section reference (e.g. 7.3). There are a number of references to two books which might usefully be followed up. *The Macmillan Casebook for 'Henry V'*, ed. Michael Quinn (1969) is indicated by the letter 'C' followed by the page number (e.g. C.37); the account of *The Royal Shakespeare Company's Production of 'Henry V' for the Centenary Season at the Royal Shakespeare Theatre*, ed. Sally Beauman (1976), is indicated by the letter 'B' with the page number following (e.g. B.201).

Cover illustration: portrait of *Henry V* by an unknown artist, reproduced by kind permission of the National Portrait Gallery. The drawing of the Globe Theatre is by courtesy of Alec Pearson.

1 SHAKESPEARE'S LIFE AND THEATRE

1.1 SHAKESPEARE'S ORIGINS

It is sometimes said that we don't know a great deal about Shakespeare's life. It is even suggested that someone of modest background and without benefit of a university education could not possibly be the author of the plays which appeared under the name 'William Shakespeare' during his lifetime and which, seven years after his death, were collected together by two life-long friends into a single folio (1623). In fact, we know a very great deal about Shakespeare, especially as compared with other dramatists of that time who wrote outstanding plays but who are little more than shadows – Webster and Tourneur, for example. If we jump ahead nearly four centuries, a handy comparison might be made with a twentieth-century author about whom we might expect to know all. Yet, for example, there are surprisingly large gaps in our knowledge of George Orwell's time in Burma and Paris from 1922 to 1929.

Shakespeare was one of a small group of close intimates, many of whom were fellow-sharers in the dramatic company for which he wrote and acted. Ben Jonson, the second most renowned dramatist of the time, knew Shakespeare well for two to three decades. It is extremely unlikely that those who worked with Shakespeare daily in London, visited Court with him to present plays, toured with him, and shared his free time, could over so long a period have been deceived by an imposter, especially as from time to time he almost certainly had to adapt his plays for special purposes at short notice (for example, *Richard III* whilst on tour of south-east England in 1597). What causes some people to question that William Shakespeare was the author of the plays and poems credited to him, apart from mere snobbishness (and it is noticeable that nearly a score of the claimants are of noble, even royal, birth), is the difficulty of comprehending how *any* such man, whose background is, paradoxically, rather well-known, could be a genius. How could this provincial grammar-school boy, with seemingly no special advantages, prove so knowledgeable, so aware, so sensitive to trends political and social, and above all, so poetic? We cannot know the answer, not because we don't know enough about William Shakespeare, but because we cannot comprehend genius. Perhaps the fact that over fifty people have been thrust forward as 'the author, William Shakespeare' is itself a measure of the weakness of such claims. Though we cannot fill in every detail of Shakespeare's life, recent research has provided hints that fill out what can be said with certainty.

William Shakespeare was baptized on 26 April 1564 at Stratford-upon-Avon and he died there 52 years later on 23 April 1616. Traditionally, his date of birth is adduced as also having been 23 April – St George's Day – and it is celebrated annually on that day in Stratford by an international gathering of diplomats, scholars, and well-wishers. His father, John, was probably quite a wealthy man, more so than has sometimes been suspected if recent research by Professor Ernst Honigmann proves to be correct. John Shakespeare was High Bailiff (= Mayor) of Stratford when his son was four and though he faced prosecution in London for illegal wool trading and usury (which lends a certain poignancy to *The Merchant of Venice*), it may have been his adherence to the Roman Catholic faith rather than financial difficulties that led to his absenting himself from his civic duties.

William Shakespeare probably went to Stratford Grammar School for some seven to eight years and although it is conventional to talk of his having 'little Latin and less Greek' it would doubtless have got him a university place in our day. He married Anne Hathaway (whose family home still survives) by special licence when he was 18½, their first child, Susanna, being born six months later. Two years after that, twins were born, Hamnet (who died when he was eleven, early in August, 1596) and Judith (so when writing *The Comedy of Errors* he had first-hand knowledge of twins). Nothing is known about the happiness or otherwise of their marriage though conjecture is rife, partly because Shakespeare left Anne 'only' their second-best bed in his will. This conjecture is based on a modern misunderstanding of that bequest. According to the law at that time, Shakespeare had no need to mention Anne at all in his will as the law clearly defined her rights. Thus, mention of *this* bed suggests it had a particular association for them which husband (and wife) wished to ensure was not forgotten.

What we know and guess of Shakespeare's early life at Stratford varies from legend, that he was caught poaching deer, to incidental events that might throw a little light on his creative genius, such as the death by drowning (a suspected suicide) in the Avon of Katharine Hamlet in 1579, calling to mind Ophelia's fate in the play, *Hamlet*. The most interesting conjecture is that he became a schoolmaster. This has recently been thoroughly re-examined by Professor Honigmann. Although it cannot be proved, he presents a fairly convincing case for suggesting that Shakespeare began his working life as an assistant schoolmaster at about the age of fifteen for Thomas Hoghton, a member of a leading Roman Catholic family in Lancashire, and then, from 1581 to 1582, for another such Lancashire family, the Heskeths. At this time Professor Honigmann believes William was, like his father, a Roman Catholic. He then returned to Stratford about August 1582, married Anne, and probably worked for his father until after the twins were born in February 1585. During that time he probably became a Protestant, whether out of conviction or convenience we cannot tell.

By 1592 we can be sure Shakespeare had some reputation as a dramatist because of the scurrilous references to him in Robert Greene's *Groats-worth of Wit*. There he is described as an 'upstart Crow, beautified with our feathers' (i.e. he has plagiarised our work), and as having 'a Tiger's hart wrapped in a Player's hide . . . the only Shake-scene in the country'. When Shakespeare arrived in London, and how he worked his way into an actors' company (little easier then than now), is not known. Professor Honigmann suggests an earlier date than usual – perhaps as early as 1585 – for his joining Lord Strange's Men. (At this time, every company of actors had to have a patron or protector.) That company was amalgamated for a time with the Admiral's Men (a company whose leading actor, Edward Alleyn, founded Dulwich College), but it eventually became the Chamberlain's Men in 1594. We know that Shakespeare was a member of that company from soon after its foundation and he remained a member until his retirement. In the pre-1590 years, Shakespeare probably wrote his two 'schoolmasterly' plays, *Titus Andronicus* and *The Comedy of Errors*; he also began his series of history plays with the three parts of *Henry VI*.

1.2 THE LORD CHAMBERLAIN'S COMPANY

Quite apart from Shakespeare's membership, the Lord Chamberlain's Company had two other claims to fame. Its position as the leading company in London meant that it often performed at Court. When involved, quite unwittingly, in putting on a special performance of Shakespeare's *Richard II* the day before the Earl of Essex's attempted coup on 7 February 1601, it had friends enough to be absolved of malice, though Essex was executed 2½ weeks later. Essex, it has been suggested, inspired aspects of plays as different as *Henry V* (see the direct reference to him in Act V, Chorus, 29–35) *Richard II* and *Hamlet*. The coming together of English, Welsh, Scotch and Irish in *Henry V* may have been inspired by a policy advocated by Essex. But perhaps the greatest interest the company has for us as a company is that it was a remarkably successful actor's co-operative. The company was not owned by some theatrical impresario (as was the Admiral's Men), and therefore at his mercy, but was owned by its leading actors, known as sharers, and it maintained a successful existence for half a century. Shakespeare almost certainly made his small fortune as a sharer in this company rather than from the money he earned by acting or writing.

1.3 THE STRATFORD GENTLEMAN

If Shakespeare spent most of his working life in London, for that was where the work was, he retained his connections with Stratford. He was wealthy enough to buy New Place, the second biggest house in the town, for his family in 1597. This cost £60, the equivalent of the amount regularly paid at this time for writing ten plays. He lived at New Place from 1611, when he retired from full-time work in London, until his death in 1616. The house was demolished in 1702.

In 1596, Shakespeare's father, probably with his son's assistance, was awarded a coat-of-arms and the right to call himself 'gentleman'. The coat-of-arms, with its motto, 'non sanz droict' (not without right), is often emblazoned on editions of Shakespeare's works. Some of his colleagues might have found this rather pretentious. Ben Jonson, though a good friend, gives the motto to Sogliardo's coat-of-arms in *Every Man in his Humour* (1599) as 'not without mustard', and that seems to be a joke at Shakespeare's expense.

Although hedged about with uncertainties, we know sufficient of Shakespeare to be able to describe him not only as the prime genius of the theatre, but also as a very shrewd and successful businessman, able to move with ease in many walks of society, rooted in his home town, not without aspirations to social advancement, but with many friends, especially his greatest rival, Ben Jonson. Even years after his death, none valued him and his work more than his fellow actors and that, in a profession not without its rivalries and petty jealousies, is in itself remarkable.

2 THE HISTORICAL BACKGROUND

2.1 HISTORICAL PERSPECTIVES

There are two dimensions to the historical background to *Henry V*. There is the history of the reign of Henry V and, in particular, Henry's first expedition to France which ended in the victory of Agincourt, and there is the history contemporaneous with Shakespeare's own life. Perhaps we should bear in mind a third historical dimension: that provided by our own experience. We 'see' Shakespeare's *Henry V* not as a detached, isolated, work of art. We come to it through what we understand of the world about us. It is easy to see how different that can be for those of different generations living today. Henry's appeal will almost certainly be very different for those of twenty or less years than it evidently was for Laurence Olivier and those of this generation when Olivier made his film version of *Henry V* during the last years of the 1939–45 War. We 'see' through our own experience and it is natural that Shakespeare did the same.

2.2 SHAKESPEARE'S SOURCES

Shakespeare's main source for *Henry V* was the second edition of Raphael Holinshed's *Chronicles* (1587) but he also read, and seems to have known well, Edmund Halle's history (1548), which was a main source for Holinshed. These provided the meat and sometimes the very words for Shakespeare's history plays, though he did not restrict himself to them, nor was he restricted by them. Shakespeare did not hesitate to reorganise the materials of history to suit his dramatic purpose, though he remained true to the spirit of the history he knew, especially that of Halle. Quite often Shakespeare's facts are wrong (e.g. the casualty figures at Agincourt) but frequently this arises from errors in his sources.

What Shakespeare shared with Halle and Holinshed was an *attitude* to history. History was, to take the title of a collection of biographies in verse well-known to Shakespeare, *A Mirror for Magistrates*. In the first edition (1559), this book is described, not as an entertainment, or as a work of art for its own sake, but as 'a mirror for all men as well noble as others, to show the slippery deceits of the wavering lady and the due regard for all kinds of vices'. The wavering lady is Dame Fortune, and fortune is fickle. History, the Elizabethans believed, taught direct lessons. It taught how to behave; it illustrated the effects of moral choices; it showed how and why men and women rose to power and how it was that they fell – how the Wheel of Fortune turned, lifting them up and then casting them down; it preached 'good order' and the duties of subjects to their rulers (monarchs and their representatives, the magistrates), and the duty of all to God. And history, it argued, repeated itself – a cliché we still sometimes hear.

Thus, Halle, Holinshed, and other historians were not just recording the past; they were warning their readers about the future, not in terms of prophecy (any more than George Orwell's *Nineteen Eighty-Four* prophesies events of that year), but how things will turn out if wrong courses are pursued (which *is* the aim of Orwell's novel).

Shakespeare, therefore, in the main read his history through Tudor interpreters who saw history as demonstrating that the deposition of God's annointed, Richard II, led to civil strife which, after nearly a century of much disorder, had been resolved by 'the Tudor Settlement'. That settlement was political and religious – the two were not divisible – and that meant, if order were to be maintained, a Protestant established church, a clear pattern of 'degree' (everyone and everything in its correct, assigned position in the great scheme of the universe), and implicit obedience.

2.3 ORDER AND OBEDIENCE

No lesson was more insistently taught in England in the sixteenth century than the need for obedience. Only by obedience would order and social stability be achieved, and hovering over all was the dread shadow of the civil war and general turbulence of the fifteenth century. Although Queen Elizabeth and her ministers undoubtedly achieved order and obedience, the lessons taught were not acquiesced in passively. There were tensions within Elizabethan society and questions asked, religious and political. But the exhortations (the word officially used) to obedience never ceased and set homilies on obedience were regularly read in churches up and down the land. This is vividly shown in the homily *Against Disobedience and Wilful Rebellion* of 1571 (when Shakespeare was seven). This is a typical passage:

> He that nameth rebellion nameth not a singular and only sin, as is theft, robbery, murder and such like; but he nameth the whole puddle and sink of all sins against God and man, against his prince, his country, his countrymen, his parents, his children, his kinsfolks, his friends, and against all men universally. All sins, I say, against God and all men heaped together, nameth he that nameth rebellion.

Yet – always yet – there was a lingering doubt. Must one be obedient if orders were neither just nor honest? An earlier Exhortation admitted that orders contrary to God's commandments need not be obeyed. This can be found reflected in Williams's anxious questioning of the king in IV.i (see pp. 41—2). So although there can be little doubt that Shakespeare accepted the degree and order of Elizabethan England, he does reflect, in *Henry V* and in other plays, questionings and uncertainties.

Shakespeare writes within a Christian framework, more established Protestant than Roman Catholic, though not without touches of the latter. That framework implies an all-prescient Providence within which men and women have free will to decide their destiny, the outcome of which God has foreseen. Therefore, making the right choices matters and that also informs *Henry V* – the king, his soldiers and officers, the church leaders, the French, and the traitors.

2.4 INFLATION AND DEARTH

There is far more to the background of Shakespeare's time than can be encompassed in this short review, but a few brief points might be helpful.

The ninety years from 1530 to 1640 was a time of serious inflation. Prices rose by five times in this period and by the time Shakespeare wrote *Henry V*, real wages were two-thirds of what they had been in 1530. From 1594 to 1602 there was a succession of bad harvests and the dearth in 1597 was particularly serious. As well as hunger, there was plague. It was bad in 1592, 1593, and 1594. In 1593 some 11 000 of London's 200 000 inhabitants succumbed; in 1603 (ironically called 'The Wonderful Year' by the dramatist and pamphleteer, Thomas

Dekker), some 38 000 of London's population died of plague. Despite such hardship and death, England's population rose from about three million to four million during the sixteenth century, the population of London increasing disproportionately from about 50 000 to 200 000. The wretchedness in which so many people then lived in England we see reported on our television screen but set today in Africa. For physical reasons alone, never mind doubts about how peace and stability were to be preserved when Queen Elizabeth died, together with religious, political, and intellectual uncertainties, there were reasons enough for the last years of the sixteenth century being a time of doubt and even depression.

2.5 SCIENTIFIC, LITERARY, AND TECHNICAL DEVELOPMENTS

Nevertheless, the sixteenth century was also a time of geographic exploration, commercial expansion, scientific investigation, rediscovery of the cultures of Ancient Greece and Rome, religious inquiry, literary and theatrical creativity (it saw the rise of the professional drama), and, perhaps most significant of all, 'the coming of the book'. In the sixteenth century publication by printing burgeoned and that led to a vast increase in the number of readers. And what people then read in England was 'serious': The Bible, of course, sermons, and religious commentaries and discussions were particularly popular. Two preachers, Henry Smith and William Perkins, had over 250 editions of their works published over a period of fifty years. In this time, ninety editions of Shakespeare's works appeared, just over thirty of Marlowe's, and a score of Spenser's. The Elizabethan had no lack of food for thought.

We can, therefore, feel pretty certain that the serious issues raised in *Henry V* interested most of its audiences and not just the most learned among them. We now also believe that the low comedy, sometimes dismissed as being just for the groundlings, was enjoyed by a wide cross-section of the audience. The special, dark, even sour, comedy of *Henry V* might well have been much better appreciated by the generality of Shakespeare's first audiences than it is by those in our allegedly more sophisticated times. Indeed, it can be suggested with some confidence that it was only Shakespeare's own audiences which were intellectually and emotionally equipped to respond with justice to the complex tensions of *Henry V*. Modern audiences require – or at least, are deemed to require – something less rigorous.

3 FROM CHRONICLE TO HISTORY PLAY

3.1 THE POPULARITY OF THE HISTORY PLAY

Shakespeare was not exceptional in finding the genre of history play attractive. Something like 20 per cent of the plays written in the last two decades of the sixteenth century were history and chronicle plays. Of the eighteen or so plays written by Shakespeare up to and including *Henry V*, half were English history plays. He continued to write history plays after *Henry V*, but only one, *Henry VIII*, had an English subject. The implications of dramatised history were very direct to the Elizabethans. The Queen herself saw Shakespeare's *Richard II* as dramatising her own feared deposition and almost a hundred years later, Charles II, not the most restrictive of monarchs, personally banned that play.

The fascination for dramatising history, though particularly strong at this time (perhaps because, consciously or unconsciously, people sought in historical examples answers to current discontents), was not peculiar to the Elizabethans. One of the earliest tragedies, *The Persians*, by Aeschylus (472 BC), is a history play and the genre was not unknown to the Romans, though Seneca's *Octavia* is the only surviving example. Today we still enjoy the genre, if more often in the cinema or on television than in the theatre, though there are notable exceptions: Robert Bolt's *A Man for All Seasons*, John Osborne's *Luther*, and, on the Continent, Bertolt Brecht's *Mother Courage*.

3.2 THE CHARACTERISTICS OF THE HISTORY PLAY

One reason for the fascination of the history play is that, if well done, it marries two irreconcilables. Just as does a metaphysical conceit in the poetry of John Donne, two conflicting modes are forced into a relevant relationship. History, ideally, is a record of what actually happened: what was done by real people at specific times, with results that may still directly affect the lives of members of the audience. It is REAL in a total sense, at least as it is ideally conceived to be. Often, of course, as in Halle and Holinshed, the record is inaccurate, incomplete, and prejudiced. Drama, however, especially before the mid-nineteenth century and the advent of Realism and Naturalism, did not pretend to be 'real' in its externals; it did not pretend to imitate actuality. It was very late in the nineteenth century that an astonished audience in Paris was treated to real kitchen chairs etc – particularly real in that the director had trundled them through the Paris streets on a cart from his mother's kitchen. And, of course, what was spoken on the sixteenth-century stage was, in the main, verse: it was not naturalistic drama. Indeed, a critic could speak of the language as 'the poem'. Long before the symbolist movements of the late nineteenth and early twentieth centuries, late medieval and Tudor dramatists fully understood the symbolic. Shakespeare as late as 1610 could use the figure of Time; Ben Jonson, in his masque, *Time Vindicated*, seven years after Shakespeare's death, used characters called Eyes, Nose, and Ears – just as Tristan Tzara would in his Dada play, *The Gas Heart*, three hundred years later. What was novel in the 1920s was, ironically, 'natural' to Shakespeare, Jonson and their audiences.

Thus, when historical drama was initiated in England in the 1530s by Bishop John Bale in his *King John*, there were 'real' characters – King John, Stephen Langton, Cardinal Pandulphus, and the Pope, for example – and symbolic 'characters' such as Widow England, Sedition, Civil Order and Private Wealth. Further, for practical purposes, it was necessary for one actor to play more than one role; the actors presenting such plays earned a living by acting and they could not collect enough money to afford the large casts used for the medieval mystery plays given by amateurs. Bale, a fierce Protestant propagandist, made a virtue of necessity and carefully arranged at least some of the doubling so that the Pope and Usurped Power were played by the same actor. That King John in this play was understood to be 'real', but is not historically correct, can easily be seen from Bale's manipulation of this role. Whether or not John was as bad as oversimple histories claim, he was certainly not the Protestant Martyr of Bale's play. This illustrates a special asset of the history play for the propagandist. Was not that King John before our eyes? Must this not have been how he truly was? If that seems naive, ask whether we truly know what happened after watching television programmes that combine fact and fiction (the sub-genre 'faction') in presenting accounts of current events that have taken place on either side of the Atlantic. T. S. Eliot, incidentally, was to use Bale's doubling technique for the Four Tempters and the Four murderous Knights in 1935 in his history play, *Murder in the Cathedral*.

Not long after Bale's *King John*, Halle's and Holinshed's histories were published, providing a rich quarry for dramatists. Much of what was written out of them for the stage was dramatically ramshackle, a loosely-linked pageant of events usually described, like their sources, as chronicle plays. The story of Henry V, as prince and king, had already been dramatised before Shakespeare started on his cycle of plays on the same subject. Thus, *The Famous Victories of Henry V*, an anonymous play, is very much in the chronicle tradition. It races through the events to which Shakespeare devotes over 10 000 lines in a mere 1400 – considerably less than Shakespeare's shortest play. It is a poor play, a bad play, but it isn't difficult to see why it entranced its first audiences and it still has a few moments of life.

3.3 SHAKESPEARE AND THE HISTORY PLAY

Shakespeare seems to have taken hold of the chronicle tradition, to have at once grasped its dramatic and thematic possibilities, and to have moulded it into a near-perfect form from the outset, even before Marlowe had written his *Edward II*, perhaps the only history play of this period seriously to rival any of Shakespeare's. Whereas other authors, dramatists and poets were content to recount the 'fall of princes' and the 'turn of Fortune's Wheel', Shakespeare dramatised the movement of history itself and in those histories calling for such an approach, showed the tragic potentiality of the fall of a prince. One of the most remarkable achievements of the four plays of which *Henry V* is the culmination – *Richard II, 1* and *2, Henry IV*, and *Henry V* (the second of Shakespeare's two groups of four history plays, or 'tetralogies' as they are termed) – is that we seem to experience a shift from a medieval to a modern world. Historically this is not correct; Henry IV and Henry V were as much medieval monarchs as was Richard II, and we really only consider modern history beginning with the Tudors: historical perspective was only slowly coming to be understood in the sixteenth century. However, in showing this change in sensibilities from those that mark Richard as medieval, to those that betoken Henry V as, in a sense, modern, Shakespeare dramatises an essential shift with great skill and insight.

Although the end of Elizabeth's reign was the high point of the English history play, the genre continued until the closing of the theatres in 1642. Roman history and myth often had to stand in for English history in order to avoid incurring the censor's wrath. Thus, the Divine Right of Kings and the legality of deposing a king, subjects dramatised by Shakespeare in the second tetralogy, keep recurring in the first forty years of the seventeenth century. There is no doubt that to audiences for a hundred years after Bale, the history play was an important means of dramatising (and discussing) issues of great moment. We should, therefore, not be surprised to find that *Henry V*, for its first audiences, was much more than a jingoistic conclusion to its tetralogy, as authors and critics as distinguished as George Bernard Shaw have mistakenly believed.

3.4 CHARACTER AND HISTORY

Characters are not to be picked out of plays like plums out of a pudding – or rather, they will resist such abstraction if a play is well written and closely integrated, as is *Henry V*. This problem is well epitomised by the kinds of poetry given by Shakespeare to the king (see Section 6). The varieties of the king's poetry are more often related to the different contexts in which it is spoken than expressive of his character. Nowhere is this more clearly to be seen than in his chilling address to the Governor and people of Harfleur (III.iii) where what is said is 'depersonalised'. It is a sort of 'Chorus speech' and might be compared from this point of view with Gertrude's 'There is a willow grows aslant a brook' in *Hamlet* (IV.vii.166–83). Were that related to character it would demand the question, 'If Gertrude saw Ophelia drowning, why did she not intervene?' Nevertheless, the characters and their representation in *Henry V* present some extremely interesting problems which can be tackled in isolation.

First and foremost, many of the play's characters were real, historical people; there was a Bishop of Ely and a Henry Chichele, Archbishop of Canterbury, but the latter's role in the play, which reflects upon his character, making him more political manipulator than pious cleric, is not historical (see I.i and I.ii); Scroop, Grey and Cambridge were historical but the device by which they are made to sign their own death warrants is not, and thus the narrative, and their characters, are modified to suit Shakespeare's thematic concerns (II.ii). The French are characterised as boastful, ill-prepared, vain, and cowardly, which hardly does them historical justice. Conversely the English lords are uniformly 'noble' in rank and behaviour at Agincourt and historic events cannot quite sustain this (see note on

York, IV.viii). All these characters are modified – distorted – to suit the story and its first audiences.

Few characters in the play are more immediately distinctive than the four Captains (III.i). Fluellen's loyalty, choleric temper, and his magnanimity, give him genuine individuality. Taken as a group, however, the four Captains, for all the differences of accent and attitude, are stereotypes. They have to be made comic (all except, perhaps, the English Captain) for extra-dramatic reasons. Two represented 'enemy' countries to the Elizabethans and the third was from a country barely assimilated. Only through comedy could Shakespeare dramatise a concept of a 'United Kingdom' which would only take political form many decades after his death (see 10.5). Character must thus be subservient to dramatic function.

It is in the character who dominates the play, Henry V, that Shakespeare's characterisation is to be seen at its most fascinating, for he had many problems to resolve, not all of them dramatic. He was not solely faced with making an historical personage interesting dramatically. Not only did he create a character fierce yet capable of being gentle, courageous yet capable of suffering, someone apart as a king yet attempting close fellowship with ordinary men, but he did this in the context of Henry's earlier dramatic heritage, which Shakespeare had himself so vividly portrayed.

From 'young wanton' to a 'gallant, Christian king'

One of the attractions that Henry V held for Elizabethans was the way that a 'young wanton and effeminate boy', as his father described him in *Richard II* (V.iii.10), proceeded through profligate youth, via seemingly miraculous conversion, to ideal king. Henry is, he claims, 'no tyrant, but a Christian king' (I.ii.241) and to Gower, at a moment when we might be tempted to suspect irony but where there is probably none, Henry is 'a gallant king' (IV.vii.10). It was a story that bore much retelling. Shakespeare himself, in parts one and two of *Henry IV*, has Hal reform and win his father's approval twice over. This might be folklorist repetition, and that would not be inappropriate, as the legendary stories of Hal's wild youth seem to have no basis in recorded fact. It is quite possible that Shakespeare was unaware that at the time Prince Henry was living so wantonly, according to legend, he was in fact closely involved, first in fighting the Welsh under Glendower and then, from 1408 to 1412, with finance and foreign policy.

However, there is some basis in Hal's apartness from his father and it serves good dramatic and political functions. Henry IV was a usurper. His son obliquely recalls this just before Agincourt

(IV.I.298–300). Hal is shown as playing no part at his father's Court. In a curious way (which more than one psychologist has convincingly explained), Hal for a time finds in Falstaff a substitute father. In *1 Henry IV* they not only play-act together but perform and exchange the roles of father and son. Falstaff, much to the annoyance of sentimentalists, cannot sustain the role of father. He may represent much that gives life its warmth, humanity, and spice, but he is essentially evil – the Vice, as Hal himself calls him, a reverend Vice maybe, but yet Iniquity. Nor does Hal ever do anything but make it categorically plain to Falstaff that his days are numbered.

Triangles of choice

The reason for Falstaff's rejection, in dramatic, political, and moral terms, is simple and it is a wayward critic or stage director who would try to distort our judgement otherwise. Shakespeare inherited a morality-play 'triangle of forces' in which Everyman had to choose between good and evil. At first he chose evil – to enjoy himself with no thought of death and judgement. He was seduced by a character generically called the Vice but often given specific names such as those Hal calls Falstaff. At the last moment, when death calls on him, he might belatedly seek the narrow path to heaven with the help of a representative of good. Marlowe uses this tradition in an ambiguous way in his *Dr Faustus*, the advice of the Good and Evil Angels being less clear-cut than at first sight appears. Traditionally, the character playing the Vice was also the company's principal comic actor and his task was not only to seduce the 'hero' but also, through his comedy, the audience. Falstaff, of course, admirably performs that task!

In *1 Henry IV*, the Good and Bad Angels are replaced by Hotspur and Falstaff – with differences. Like the Angels in *Dr Faustus*, neither is wholly good nor wholly bad. Hal's father wishes his son were like Hotspur, even imagining some fairy had exchanged the babies in their cradles (see 3.5). Hal's task is not, as in a morality play, to choose one or other of Hotspur or Falstaff, but to find his way between them, taking from each what is honourable and human respectively, and rejecting what is worthless. He must seek personal integrity rather than the empty honour for which Hotspur would give all, yet not rejecting, as does Falstaff, all that is honourable.

In a more complex way the pattern is again followed in *2 Henry IV* so that by the end of each play, the Prince has discovered something of his true self; he is not tarred with his father's usurpation; has discovered something of the nature of life as it is ordinarily lived; but has rejected the meanness and greed which, as much as fun and warmth, too obviously characterize Falstaff. Despite having learned so much, he knows on ascending the throne that there is still much to be learned and, symbolically, he is reconciled with the Lord Chief Justice who will be his new guiding spirit (though he does not appear in *Henry V*).

Of course, we should look at plays as individual works of art, but this tetralogy is, despite a few contradictions, so intimately bound together, so much of a piece, that some awareness of what happens in each play is essential to understanding the individual plays. What is more, Shakespeare seems to go out of his way to draw attention to some of the links between the plays. No Elizabethan audience would come to *Henry V* unaware of what Shakespeare had dramatised in the three earlier plays of the series.

The ideal ruler

Henry V is, of course, concerned with the events leading up to a battle and the surprising victory its hero achieves. It is also concerned with a personal conflict which is also crowned with a surprising victory, surprising if one looks back to Henry IV's description of his son as a 'wanton and effeminate boy'. (Effeminate here means self-indulgent.) What Prince Hal has learned in the earlier plays is tested in *Henry V*. Further, Shakespeare sets up Henry against the pattern of an ideal ruler. In great detail, John Walter has itemised in his *Introduction to the New Arden Shakespeare* (reprinted C 132–4), what the sixteenth century, through the treatises of Erasmus and Chelidonius, believed made an ideal monarch. Thus, for example, he should be a Christian, show no clemency to those who would injure the state, take no personal revenge, be counselled by wise men, be familiar with the humble but not corrupted by them, execute or banish parasites, and consider his responsibility for the deaths of the innocent in war. Such a king would find that the cares of state hinder sleep; he would regard ceremony and royal insignia as valueless in themselves; and even the commonwealth of the bees (I.ii.187–204) is described in these treatises on the ideal monarch. It is easy to see how closely Shakespeare works-in these (and other) qualities and characteristics.

Henry V as dramatic character

At one level, Shakespeare dramatises in *1* and *2 Henry IV* the transformation of a young wanton to a responsible ruler and then, in *Henry V*, tests him against the pattern of an ideal monarch. Had Shakespeare left it at that – and some critics and directors take the play no further than that – the result just might have earned the opprobrium heaped on Henry (and Shakespeare) by antipathetic critics. A Poet Laureate, John Masefield, thought him 'the one commonplace man in the eight [history] plays' (C. 42). Bernard Shaw thought Shakespeare could hardly be forgiven 'for the worldly phase in which he tried to thrust such a Jingo hero as his Harry V down our throats' (C. 55) and W. B. Yeats preferred 'porcelain Richard II' to 'the vessel of clay Henry V . . . He has the gross vices, the coarse nerves, of one who is to rule among violent people' (C. 55), the extravagance of which was somewhat deflated by E. E. Stoll, who, responding to this assessment, described Yeats as 'Poet of the Celtic twilight, of them that went forth to battle but always fell' (C. 103). Not all the battles over *Henry V* were fought at Agincourt!

However, Shakespeare does not give us quite so over-simplified, so untarnished, a hero as these criticisms suggest. If he passes his test, if he wins a famous victory, Shakespeare is very conscious of the price; if we aren't, we don't read, or see, what is there to be read and staged. Samuel Johnson complained strongly about the inadequacy of the fifth act of *Henry V*: 'The great defect of this play is the emptiness and narrowness of the last act, which a very little diligence might have easily avoided' (C. 34). It is dangerous to do battle with Johnson, but here I think him wrong, and he may have led others astray, especially those anxious to get the play over once Agincourt has been won. 'The excitement's over. Let's wrap it all up and get home!' Why, we must ask, did Shakespeare go to such trouble to write a long final scene to the play, a scene not merely long, but the longest of the play? Johnson might have had in mind something he wrote in his Preface to his 1765 edition of Shakespeare's plays:

> When he found himself near the end of his work, and in view of his reward, he shortened the labour to snatch the profit. He therefore remits his efforts where he should most vigorously exert them, and his catastrophe is improbably produced or imperfectly represented.

That is, Shakespeare scamped the end of his plays in order to deliver his script and get his fee! If Johnson thought that, he might have asked why Shakespeare should have behaved so differently in composing the end of *Henry V*. The answer – *an* answer – is developed more fully elsewhere (see V.ii and 7.9), but briefly, Shakespeare, whilst maintaining Henry's epic stature also shows his less admirable traits in the last scene. As Falstaff warned the king when he was but a prince and Falstaff was play-acting the role of father-king:

There is a thing, Harry, which thou has heard of, and it is known to
many in our land by the name of pitch. This pitch . . . doth defile,
so doth the company thou keepest.

1 Henry IV (II.iv.403–6)

So too does the carnage of war and the violence it entails – the
cutting of prisoners' throats – stick like pitch and thus can Henry see
the Princess of France as 'one fair French maid that stands in my way'
and, like a 'a fair French city' to be assaulted (V.ii.336–7). Of course
if you cut this from the scene in performance, the point is lost and
then Shakespeare's carefully structured qualification of his 'ideal'
king is also lost.

3.5 **THE PATH TO AGINCOURT**

Historical motivation

Henry V made not one but three expeditions to France. The first two
are represented in Shakespeare's play; the third ended with Henry's
death from dysentery. The play outlines reasons for the first invasion
at some length. These closely follow Holinshed's *Chronicles* but
Holinshed was partly in error. The characters most misrepresented in
this explanation are the Archbishop, Henry Chichele, who was not
present but, ironically, probably serving in France as Ambassador to
the French Court; and the Dauphin. Shakespeare, as not infrequently, deliberately or not, gets the ages of his characters wrong.
Thus in *1 Henry IV*, the king speaks of his son and Hotspur being
babies at the same time. In fact, Hotspur was three years older than
Henry IV himself and twenty-three years older than Hal! In this play,
the Dauphin's gibe at Henry V's youth (I.ii.250) comes oddly from a
man nine years younger than the king. In 1414, Henry was 27 and the
Dauphin 18. There *was* an anecdote current then that the Dauphin
had insulted Henry with a gift of tennis balls, but that, according to
Peter Saccio, seems to have been a propagandist reworking of an
ancient insult King Darius of Persia gave the young Alexander the
Great (a monarch, incidentally, who features prominently in act IV
scene vii). Shakespeare's sources were also unreliable in giving the
clerics selfish motives for financing the invasion. The Church did
contribute, much as was customary, but urging the king to invade was
not designed to head off a bill in Parliament to dispossess the Church
of its lands. That bill had been tabled in Henry IV's reign; it was not
proceeded with in the reign of Henry V.

Henry's motivation in invading France was twofold. By far the most important consideration was his duty, as medieval and renaissance rulers and theoreticians would understand it, in claiming and holding that which was properly his kingdom by dynastic right. That would seem to Elizabethans (and Henricians) not merely a natural claim but a first demand on a monarch's attention. Alberico Gentili, the 16th-century founder of international law and the author of three books on the law of war, wrote:

> as the kings of England wished to retain their rights in the kingdom of France . . . calling themselves their kings . . . and thus they preserve a kind of civil possession . . . And that title is not an empty one . . . (C.141)

In effect, after three centuries, the tables had been turned on France. Having invaded England in 1066, imposed their language and customs on the Anglo-Saxons, the descendants of French rulers, especially Edward III and Henry V, became powerful enough as Kings of England to seek to claim lands whence their forefathers came by right of descent. This said, modern audiences (and directors) are quickly bored by dynastic arguments which Elizabethans found fascinating and so cutting is inevitable. Elizabethans, for their part, might find our obsession with a contemporary TV series involving family relationships - such as *Dynasty* – trivial.

In a curious way, the legal argument upon which Henry's claim was based, and resisted by the French, is not without parallel in Europe today. We are no longer quite so concerned with dynastic claims to territory, though they do recur, but members of the EEC are still quite good at changing the ground rules to suit national convenience (by redefining health regulations, for example) to hinder imports which should be allowed free entry. At the root of the argument in *Henry V*, was the fact that whereas the English allowed a woman to be their crowned monarch – as was Elizabeth I at the time Shakespeare wrote the play – the French did not. The French had changed 'the rules' early in the fourteenth century to accommodate their needs. Now, in the light of Henry V's claim, which went back to his grandfather, Edward III, the French changed the rules again, arguing that a woman might not even transmit a claim to the French crown. That this did not apply in England was to be demonstrated a few years after *Henry V* was written when James VI of Scotland became James I of England by right of descent from an aunt of Queen Elizabeth. We should not be too quick to regard such international disputation as antiquated; only the subject matter has changed.

Henry's route

Henry's three campaigns took place in 1415 in the area between Le Havre and Calais, never moving very far inland; from 1417 to 1420 in Normandy; and from 1421 to 1422 in the area between the Marne and the Loire. The second campaign was concluded by the Treaty of Troyes, one provision of which was the marriage of Henry and Katharine, and that ends Shakespeare's play; however, only the first campaign is dramatised. It might be of interest to plot out the route taken by Henry's army in 1415. Apart from helping to relate events, it is an area which a great many more peaceful British invaders have come to know well in recent decades. Two aspects of the route are particularly worth noting. First, Henry was forced to make a wide detour in order to find a place to cross the River Somme. Second, Agincourt was fought but a few miles from Edward III's triumph at Crécy in 1346.

The area around Agincourt, Picardy and Artois, together with Flanders and Brabant to the north (now part of Belgium), were subject to the Duke of Burgundy, the 'peacemaker' of act V, scene ii.

The wretchedness of the march from Harfleur to Agincourt is well described by Holinshed, who also gives at this point in his chronicle an account of the stealing of a pyx and the punishment of the offender (see III.vi):

> The Englishmen were brought into some distress in this journey, by reason of their victuals in manner spent, and no hope to get more; for the enemies had destroyed all the corn before they came. Rest could they none take, for their enemies with alarms did ever so infest them. Daily it rained and nightly it froze; of fuel there was great scarcity, of fluxes plenty; money enough, but wares for their relief to bestow it on had they none. Yet in this great necessity, the poor people of the country were not spoiled, nor anything taken of them without payment nor any outrage or offence done by the Englishmen, except one which was that a soldier took a pyx out of a church, for which he was apprehended and the king not once removed till the box was restored and the offender strangled.

It is not difficult to trace the route of the English army on a map of Northern France. It began to invest Harfleur, a little to the north of Le Havre, on 17 August 1415. The town capitulated on 22 September but the army did not move off until 7 October. It marched a little inland, bypassing Dieppe, until it reached the mouth of the River Somme on 13 October. It then worked its way upstream until a place could be found to cross the river near Nesle on 19 October. The army then marched downstream towards the coast until 23 October, when, some twenty miles from the coast, it turned towards Calais. Henry crossed the River Ternoise on 23 October and the Battle of Agincourt was fought on the 25th. Calais was reached on 29 October but the army did not embark for Dover until 17 November. It was back in London on 23 November, some five months after setting out on 18 June.

4 SUMMARY AND COMMENTARY

Prologue

Commentary

Gaining the attention of the audience in Shakespeare's day was not a simple matter of dimming the auditorium lights. For upwards of two hundred years, many plays had been started by a member of the cast addressing the would-be audience directly so ensuring their interest in the drama that was to be enacted. By the time Shakespeare wrote, plays were being performed in purpose-built theatres and that method of 'getting the play going' was no longer necessary. In *Henry V*, however, Shakespeare returns to that old technique. The play starts with the entry of a 'character' called 'Prologue', this role being played by the same actor who will also be the play's 'Chorus' (see 3.4) – our guide through the play's action. By the use of this simple, slightly obsolete, device, Shakespeare can throw his audience back into an earlier period of drama, just as if he were placing them in an earlier historical context, and also seek to control our responses to his drama. So, Prologue begins by contrasting what the subject of the play needs if it were to be dramatised adequately with the limited resources available to Shakespeare's company. Only the lively imaginations of the audience can bridge that gap. Thus, we, the audience, are to be essential collaborators in this 'action' – the action of the play and, by extension, of Agincourt.

Shakespeare employs a Chorus, or Prologue, or equivalent 'character' (such as Rumour, who speaks the Induction to *2 Henry IV*) in half-a-dozen plays, but in none, not even in *Pericles*, which makes full use of a Chorus (given the name of the poet, Gower), is the technique of Chorus used as complexly as it is in *Henry V*. The Chorus of this play, and initially the Prologue, perform double and paradoxical functions. Simultaneously they tell the audience, 'This is not real: you are only watching a play'; at the same time, however, they draw the audience into that play-world by their appeal to members of the audience that they exercise their imaginations, that they 'Piece out our imperfections with your thoughts', that they *see* what is only described, that they overleap time. It is a useful exercise to think what the effect of the play would be *without* Prologue and Chorus as a way of gauging the significance of Shakespeare's use of this old device.

Henry V might easily have been expected by its first audiences to have been 'just another chronicle play', a rag-bag, catch-all of the kind which Shakespeare had been largely instrumental in shaping into a dramatic art-form. There was indeed just such a play performed by a rival company, the Admiral's Men, in 1595, and there survives yet another version of the story of Prince Hal and King Henry V (the subject matter of three plays by Shakespeare) in a play probably dating from the early 1590s: *The Famous Victories of Henry V*. Shakespeare immediately strikes a different tone. Prologue speaks as if announcing an Epic. The assistance of the Muse of Fire, the inventive genius, is invoked. The first lines set a sense of some magnificence but soon, quite subtly, Shakespeare points to the inevitable miseries attendant upon war – 'famine, sword, and fire' (7) – and yet, at the same time, their 'status' is raised. They are to be servants to the King of England, his dogs, reined to his service. The effect is more obvious in the first printing of the Prologue in 1623 – it was omitted from the very much shortened version of the play printed in 1600. There, each of these words is given an initial capital letter as if personifying these elements. Right from the start of the play, Shakespeare 'has it both ways', as it were, and this is a technique that he will use with particular effect later in the action.

The function of the Muse in drama is very well outlined by another great poet, Alexander Pope, writing a Prologue for Addison's tragedy, *Cato*, just over a century later:

> To wake the soul by tender strokes of art,
> To raise the genius, and to mend the heart;
> To make mankind in conscious virtue bold,
> Live o'er each scene, and be what they behold:
> For this the Tragic Muse first trod the stage.

Although Pope has in mind the Muse of Tragedy, his lines might well serve as Prologue to *Henry V*. Note especially the fourth line.

The phrase, 'this wooden O', is famous far beyond its context, but it conceals an intriguing puzzle. What does the 'O' refer to? It is loosely used to suggest the theatre built and owned by Shakespeare's company of actors, the Lord Chamberlain's Men: the Globe. However, it is unlikely that it was at the Globe that *Henry V* was first performed. It was probably at the Curtain that the play was first presented, a theatre 'old' in the short time-scale of Elizabethan theatre buildings. Hence the denigration of what that theatre could provide. However, by the time *Henry V* was but a few months old, it was being played at the brand new, up-to-date, Globe Theatre, of which Shakespeare's company must have been very proud. Thus, these same words become not plain description but rather ironic: not even such a fine new theatre as this, the Globe, can do justice to *this* theme!

It is sometimes said that Chorus is in a privileged position in that he alone speaks directly to the audience whereas all the other characters are 'overheard'. This is far from true of drama in this period in general, though it is reasonably correct for *Henry V* – but see the Boy's speech in III.ii and the commentary thereon.

One final point about the theatre orientation of the play: 'cockpit' (11) refers to a place where cockfighting took place; one such arena was later adapted as a theatre, The Phoenix.

Act I, Scene i

Summary

Two topics are discussed. The clergy are concerned about a threat to the lands which have passed into their possession and which Parliament wished to take from them. The Archbishop (Chichele) proposes to offer the king a greater sum than the clergy have ever donated to finance the expedition to France in order to divert attention from the bill before Parliament. Secondly, the king's wild youth as Prince Hal, dramatised in the two parts of *Henry IV*, is recalled and especially his near-miraculous change of heart. It is to this reformed character that the Archbishop intends to describe the 'true titles' he has to certain French dukedoms and to the French crown itself.

Commentary

Shakespeare in this scene dramatises an uncomfortable aspect of what can otherwise be seen as mere patriotic display. What the Archbishop – and, of course, he was a real person, the founder of All Souls' College, Oxford – reveals is a plan to manipulate the king's new-found 'grace and fair regard', his piety. In order that the king will not seem easily duped, the Archbishop presents his case for an expedition to France as a righteous quest for true inheritance and thus almost a holy duty. It is plain to us, but not to the king, that this is being done to protect the Church's *secular* interests: its property. Shakespeare is himself here manipulating the facts of history. There was such a bill before Parliament in the preceding reign but it had not been revived in Henry V's time. Shakespeare's selection of his material and his re-arrangement of the facts of history seems designed to throw a shameful light upon the way the clerics manipulate the king's conversion for their own secular ends.

The scene betrays a technique typical of first-rate dramatic craftsmen, a technique Shakespeare reveals even in his earliest work. Thus, there is reference to the past out of which present events grew (here, the past as dramatised in earlier plays of the tetralogy); these events are taken a stage further (the dilemma in which the Church finds itself); and then we look forward to the resolution of this dilemma – Canterbury's manipulation of events. Thus the scene is almost a little three-act play in its own right and in this way there is always a sense of onward movement.

Act I, Scene ii

Summary

This scene may conveniently be divided into three. First, the Archbishop of Canterbury explains at some length the basis of the king's claim to the throne of France; then King Henry prudently considers the dangers England will face from Scotland if he invades France; finally, the French Ambassador delivers to Henry an insult from the Dauphin, the heir to the French throne: 'a tun of treasure' – to wit, tennis balls. Henry maintains a chilly control of himself, a mode to be repeated in IV.vii when, with barely suppressed anger, he receives news of the murder of the baggage boys. The scene, and the first act, end with the king's instructions to his nobles that they make all speed to prepare for the invasion of France, to 'chide the Dauphin at his father's door' (308).

Commentary

On a number of occasions Shakespeare writes what can seem inordinately long scenes in order to make his point. Prospero's opening explanation in *The Tempest* and the scene in London in *Macbeth* are well-known examples. This scene is often cut savagely. In Olivier's film, more than half is omitted but despite that, there seems a need to provide much comic business (by the Bishop of Ely) in an effort to hold the audience's attention. The scene is based closely on Shakespeare's source, Holinshed's *Chronicles*, but that is not too closely in accord with the facts. It is extremely doubtful whether the Dauphin did insult the king by a gift of tennis balls, though that story was spread about and is repeated by Holinshed; it is far more probable that Henry Chichele was in France as English Ambassador rather than at the Leicester Parliament where Holinshed has him making his 'Salic Law speech'. The lengthy explanation tends to be cut not because of doubts as to its historicity but because we take less delight in legal argument than did the Elizabethans. (It is, perhaps, worth bearing in mind that in Shakespeare's time sermons were probably the most popular form of publication and that people would stand outdoors for upwards of three hours listening to a favourite preacher.) The references to Scotland are also usually shortened or even cut in their entirety in order to avoid giving offence to the Scots. The insult from the Dauphin (and early editions spell the title, 'Dolphin', to which the word is related, the dolphin being hierarchically next to the whale, the king of fish), is designed to tax Hal's new-found maturity: will he rage or respond with childish petulance? The king effectively turns the insult back on the Dauphin, and Shakespeare contrasts the image of war as game with the inevitable effects of war: the making of widows. (Note 'the game's afoot' – meaning the battle is engaged – at III.i.30.)

Act II, Chorus

Summary
The Chorus contrasts English excitement with French fear as preparations for war are made. He then turns to the conspiracy by English traitors in the pay of the French who intend to assassinate Henry. Finally, almost as an afterthought, the Chorus seems to remember that the next scene takes place in London, not at the port of embarkation, Southampton.

Commentary
The logic of these lines is far from straightforward and most editors suspect revision of the play with consequential adaptation of Chorus's lines. The speech begins with a fine flourish, neatly contrasts the patriotic enterprise with treachery, and then begins to lose direction as if Shakespeare were uncertain of what were to be the ensuing order of events. There is another reference to the playhouse nature of what the audience is witnessing, coupled with almost coy jokes about the avoidance of sea-sickness.

Act II, Scene i

Summary

The purveyors of one strand of the play's comedy are now introduced. The most prominent of the group is Pistol, whose furious
language and exaggerated posturing provide a comic commentary on
military glory. The main concern of the scene is to prepare the
audience for Falstaff's imminent death. Shakespeare breaks the news
over two scenes, as if very cautiously warning his first audiences that
one of his most popular characters, Falstaff, will not be appearing, as
was promised at the end of the preceding play, *2 Henry IV*:

> If you be not too much cloyed with fat meat, our humble author
> will continue the story, with Sir John in it, and make you merry
> with fair Katharine of France – where, for anything I know,
> Falstaff shall die of a sweat, unless already 'a be killed with your
> hard opinions.

There was no question of Falstaff being killed with the public's 'hard
opinions'; almost certainly the actor who created the role, William
Kempe, had left the company.

Commentary

We tend to classify works of art by category. This can be helpful but it
can tend to narrow our response. Shakespeare's plays were first
issued as 'Comedies, Histories and Tragedies', although these three
genres have never proved enough for critics. Even a play as clearly a
tragedy as *Hamlet* is often comic and in several different ways. The
two plays that precede *Henry V* in this group of four are often richly
comic and it would not be unreasonable for an audience to expect
comedy in this play also. There *is* a fair amount of comedy in *Henry V*
but it is often strangely dark in tone or contrasted with the plainly
non-comic. In this scene the comedy is beset with images of violence,
disease ('the powdering-tub of infamy', 75) and sickness. It is a
pattern Shakespeare will repeat and it suggests a dimension to the
play quite different from one of simple patriotic chauvinism (see
7.3).

Act II, Scene ii

Summary

The 'three corrupted men', bribed with French money (hence the
gilt/guilt pun of the preceding Chorus, 26), are exposed. Shakespeare
takes the subject matter from his historical sources, Holinshed and
Halle, but invents a new incident: the drunkard who rails against

Henry. The king proposes to free him. Lord Scroop, Sir Thomas Grey and the Earl of Cambridge protest but so, with bitter irony, sign their own death warrants and are despatched to immediate execution (sometimes carried out on stage). The way is now clear for Henry to sail to France to claim what he has been persuaded is his own.

Commentary
The crucial lines in this scene come towards its end:

> Touching our person seek we no revenge;
> But we our kingdom's safety must so tender (175–5)

The drunkard was not introduced simply for sentimental effect to show a kinder side of Henry's character. Henry pardons him because his offence was against him personally, as a man, and could do the State no injury. He cannot reprieve the three conspirators, however, for they do threaten the stability of the State. In this way Henry exemplifies characteristics thought appropriate to the ideal king. He is prepared to show clemency if the State is not endangered (the drunkard); he will maintain the integrity of the kingdom (the invasion of France to secure 'his crown'); he does not take personal revenge but shows no mercy to those who threaten the kingdom (the conspirators). There is also dramatised an issue which will recur: the distinction between Henry as man and as king. What at first sight seems a simple bit of story-telling is full of significances especially for an Elizabethan audience (see p.16, 5.3 and 5.5).

Act II, Scene iii

Summary
Falstaff's death is announced in a mixture of pathos and comedy, after which the trio of comic characters leaves to join the king's expedition.

Commentary
The death of Falstaff would have been to its first audiences as sad a blow as if Falstaff were a real person. It is made more acceptable by the touching confusion of language with which the Hostess expresses her grief. Her second speech, as printed in most editions, contains one of the most famous, and most convincing, of all emendations to Shakespeare. The early text has 'a Table' for what the eighteenth-century scholar, Theobald, suggested should be ' 'a babbled'. Every modern editor emends the texts of Shakespeare's plays to try to

restore what he or she thinks Shakespeare would have wished to have had printed had he overseen his plays through the press.

It has been suggested that Falstaff's 'death' was made necessary because the Chamberlain's Men's leading comic actor, William Kempe, had left them. Kempe seems to have been so closely identified with the part that although he was replaced as First Comic by Robert Armin (rather than promote Kempe's partner, Richard Cowley), it is likely that Armin played Pistol rather than allow him to take over 'Kempe's Falstaff'. It is impossible to know whether when the play was first drafted Shakespeare intended a part for Falstaff before he was required to 'write him out' (just as is done in contemporary television soap serials). There are one or two 'fossils' in the dialogue which suggest that at least some of Pistol's lines were originally written for Falstaff (see V.i.85ff.).

Act II, Scene iv

Summary
The stage action shifts to France. King Charles is greatly perturbed at the prospect of the English invasion. His son, the Dauphin, is contemptuous of Henry V, thinking him still 'a vain, giddy, shallow, humorous youth' (28), as Shakespeare had dramatised him in *1 Henry IV*. The Constable of France tells the Dauphin he is mistaken: King Henry is very different from Prince Hal. English Ambassadors enter and their leader, the Duke of Exeter, King Henry's uncle, demands that King Charles surrender his crown to its rightful wearer – Henry V. He also expresses Henry's contempt for the Dauphin. Charles asks for a night to consider Henry's demand.

Commentary
One of the problems Shakespeare faced in dramatising *Henry V* in the Elizabethan theatre was how to present the battle scenes convincingly, or at least, their effect. The resources he *didn't* have available are clearly shown in Olivier's film: horses charging, hundreds of bowmen, flights of arrows, and so on. He solves this problem by building up a series of vignettes so that we shall see the battle through the experience and reactions of well-identified individuals. In this scene we see three characters being established: The Duke of Exeter, the elderly, wise adviser to the king, always at his right hand; the intelligent calmness of the Constable of France (so that his seduction by the French euphoria in IV.ii becomes the more telling); and, especially, the arrogance of the Dauphin. The conflicts inherent between these and other characters stand as proxy for the conflicts of battle. There is, as it were, a conflict of characters and attitudes

between, for example, King Henry and the Dauphin, so that we are as aware of the nature of the opposition of the one to the other, and of its outcome, as if an armed confrontation had been staged. Not only does this mean that Shakespeare can dispense with cavalry and massed archers in the theatre, but we can relate directly to the tensions between the characters he has built up.

Some productions tend to make the French king timid to the point of senility. Olivier, in his film, even had the king faint as Exeter made his parting speech, 'Despatch us with all speed' (141–3). This is to sacrifice the greater concerns of the play for a rather cheap, momentary, bit of stage business. So weak a French king is hardly worthy opposition for Henry.

Act III, Chorus

Summary
Chorus describes the departure of the royal fleet, bound for Harfleur. Despite the anxieties expressed earlier (I.ii.137–220), England is now said to be left in the care of the aged and babies. Harfleur is besieged. The French king's ambassador arrives offering peace terms: his daughter's hand in marriage with 'Some petty and unprofitable dukedoms' (31) as dowry. This the king rejects and the siege continues. 'Hampton' (for Southampton), found in most modern editions, is an eighteenth-century emendation. Shakespeare seems to have written 'Dover', having in mind the Dover-Calais route, and so 'Calais' at III.ii.47 (see p.33 below).

Commentary
Shakespeare begs his audience to 'Play with [their] fancies' and to 'work [their] thoughts', in order that they might the better imagine the shift from England to France, but he prompts these imaginings with romantic, almost hyperbolic language (see 9). Tucked away, almost obscurely, in this florid speech is the French king's counter offer. It is easy to overlook the fact that the French king made a not unreasonable offer to Henry. He could hardly be expected to offer to give up his crown, but he does offer his daughter's hand in marriage and Chorus's descriptions of the dukedoms as 'petty and unprofitable' comes from the mouth of someone with English prejudices. The positioning of this offer in the midst of the description of the siege of Harfleur, its relative weight – a mere four lines – and the way the dukedoms are described, ensure we pay the offer little attention. In fact, what is on offer before a single life has been lost in this invasion is pretty well what Henry gladly accepts at the end of the play after so much anguish and loss of life. Shakespeare incorporates

another irony in the Chorus. Two scenes earlier we have seen a trio of those who are following the king to France: Pistol, Bardolph, and Nym. In the Chorus they must be numbered among 'These culled and choice-drawn cavaliers'!

It is during this Chorus that Olivier in his film version shifts from the presentation of the play in a mock-up of the Globe Theatre (see 8.3) to a realistic representation of the action in modern film conventions.

Act III, Scene i

Summary
King Henry's invocation to his troops before the walls of Harfleur – 'Once more unto the breach . . . Or close the wall up with our English dead' – implies a final desperate effort after several assaults have been repulsed. Henry's appeal works and all follow, with the exception of the small group we shall find in the next scene.

Commentary
After Hamlet's, 'To be, or not to be', this is perhaps the most famous speech in all Shakespeare. Its rhetoric seems of a piece with the immediately preceding Chorus for it has something of the same hyperbolic quality. We have become so used to 'imitating the action of the tiger' that this image seems more rational than, in fact, it is. Look at the description of the eye (10–11). There is surely an exaggeration here that comes close to parody. The violence of the language almost does violence to the description. The final appeal, with its paralleling of war and sport ('The game's afoot', 32) strikes anyone aware of the too-frequent analogy of war and sport (as at times in the War of 1914–18) as facile. If the speech borders on dangerous exaggeration, it nevertheless has to be taken in the spirit of the circumstances that demand it. This is a desperate moment and it requires all the king's ability to whip up his troops' spirits. What saves it from going too far is its variation of tone: it is not all of a piece. Olivier, partly to cope with the conventions of film-making, suddenly dropped the force of his delivery at the third line and much of the speech was given conversational qualities. Also, instead of moving into close-up for the climax, centring on 'the star', the camera tracks backwards so that the king is seen from further and further away and it is his men who fill the screen. A stage production, of course, cannot so alter the audience's perspective, but it can offer that essential variety of tone. The audience, as much as the troops – the actors – *must* be taken along with the king: it is as if the

audience were also to be inspired to follow Harry once more into the breach.

The king's enthusiasms for attack and his likening this action to a game, suggest that, just as when he was a prince, he has something yet to learn. The full implication of the sport in which he is engaged will come with the killing of the baggage-boys. Shakespeare does not, however, wait so long to give his audience a counterbalancing point of view: it comes in the next scene.

Act III, Scene ii

Summary

The second scene of Act Three falls into two parts. Indeed, as the stage is cleared after the exit of the Boy (usually a mark of scene division in the Elizabethan theatre), it could be argued that III.ii is really two scenes, not one. However, taken as a whole, it offers a balanced contrast between the comic reprobates of the first part, reluctant to engage in the fighting, and the loyally comic national stereotypes of the second half, the two parts turning about the Boy's sober reflections upon his colleagues.

Commentary

Bardolph's first line parodies Henry's in the preceding scene. It is a remarkable undermining of the epic tradition from within the play. It should make an audience, or the reader, stand back from the action and see what is happening in a fresh perspective. Shakespeare is subtly doing something he will practise throughout the play: presenting a proud, patriotic, noble view of Henry and what he stands for and, simultaneously, questioning it. One should not be allowed to drive out the other. Bardolph is not meant to undercut the king – he is far too unworthy to carry our conviction – but his ribald use of Henry's call to arms should make us see the attack on Harfleur from a different point of view.

The Boy then ruminates on the inadequacies of those who should be setting him an example and determines to quit their service. He makes his speech directly to the audience. It is a measure of the significance that Shakespeare gives to what he says that it is dramatised in this manner. Such direct address gives a speech a special weight and conviction because of the intimate relationship it establishes between the speaker and the audience. Thus, although in the 'scale of the epic' the Boy plays but a very minor role, what he says is contrastingly much more important. The Boy's reference to Nym and Bardolph stealing a fire-shovel at Calais indicates some confusion either in the transmission of the text or, more probably, in the author's mind. In the Chorus preceding Act III the early texts speak of the expedition leaving from Dover instead of Southampton (Hampton as emended by most editors) and Shakespeare seems to have had the Dover-Calais crossing in mind. There is no doubt that Henry's fleet sailed from Southampton and thence to the mouth of the Seine; Harfleur is close by Le Havre. Thereafter his army proceeded slowly and painfully *towards* Calais, coming face to face with the French army at Agincourt some 40 miles south of Calais (now called Azincourt).

If the first part of the scene offers rather sour comedy, the badinage between the four Captains representing Wales, England, Ireland and Scotland is more lighthearted. The professional rivalry of the Captains stands in sharp contrast to the self-interest of Pistol, Bardolph and Nym. They argue about the digging of mines under Harfleur's walls in order to blow a breach in them. Macmorris is weary and frustrated, a natural bait to Fluellen's criticism, which is based on hide-bound adherence to textbook modes of waging war. The squabble comes close to violence, betraying the tensions between Henry's mixed force, and pointing to the need for, and difficulty of achieving an (inter)national unity.

It is the Boy who most stands out in this scene. His simple good sense not only 'places' the ruffians whom he has followed to France, so that we are not tempted to agree with Bardolph's parody of Henry, but is also an antidote to the bickering of the four captains. His speech is one of a number of remarkable moments in this play which only familiarity and changing social conditions have tended to make less strange. There is no evidence to link this Boy with his death when the baggage-train is plundered but it is dramatically appropriate that having been so clearly established here, he should in IV.vii be carried on-stage, dead, in the arms of one of the soldiers just prior to Henry's 'I was not angry since I came to France' (57).

Act III, Scene iii

Summary

Henry formally warns the Governor and people of Harfleur that further resistance will lead to the total destruction of their town and the rape and murder of its inhabitants. The Governor then enters. The Dauphin, he says, cannot come to their aid and so he surrenders the town to Henry. There is a hint that, despite this success, all is not well with the king's army; sickness – dysentery – is spreading through his forces.

Commentary
It can be difficult for a modern reader to come to terms with this
scene. It is not merely that Henry makes dire threats, but the
language in which they are couched is almost crudely violent.
Further, he disassociates himself from the actions he foresees should
the town not surrender. Thus:

> What is it then to me, if impious war . . .
> Do, with his smirched complexion, all fell feats
> Enlinked to waste and desolation? (15, 17–18)

And even more savage and inhuman

> What is't to me, when you yourselves are cause,
> If your pure maidens fall into the hand
> Of hot and forcing violation? (19–21)

There is, of course, something hypocritic about modern criticism
that finds Henry's speech barbaric. The appalling slaughter of
twentieth-century war (and worse, peace), makes Henry's threats,
and still more, his practice, seem gentle in comparison. It is important to get the speech into that perspective and then to consider the
framework within which Henry is speaking.

Shakespeare casts the speech in the framework of military conventions of his time. This, despite the violence of his language, was, so
far as these things can ever be, a relatively civilised code as compared to contemporary practice. A besieged town might hold out so
long in the hope of relief arriving, but, beyond that point, it would be
warned that surrender would no longer be accepted and total sack
would ensue. Henry mounted three campaigns in France; this
campaign of 1415; a campaign in Normandy that lasted from 1417 to
1420; and a final expedition of 1421–2, cut short by his death from
dysentery. Henry followed this code of practice with great effect in
his second campaign at the conclusion of which the Treaty of Troyes
was signed by which his demands were conceded and twelve days
after the Treaty was signed he married Katharine. Shakespeare
makes the surrender of Harfleur represent a major characteristic of
the first two campaigns, telescoping both campaigns into the fall of
Harfleur and the victory of Agincourt.

The half line, 'when you yourselves are cause', can seem particularly cynical. It has for us a contemporary ring as, say, Government
and Unions blame the actions each takes upon the other's intransi-
gence. Henry, however, is here reinforcing the conventional code of

practice appropriate to the conduct of sieges. After this warning, it *will* be the Governor's responsibility if his town is laid waste, its women raped and its men murdered. Nevertheless, the fierce cruelty of Henry's speech cannot be argued away nor would Shakespeare have expected that. We are to see both the hard realities of war and the hard edge of the professional soldier.

The stage directions of modern editions clarify what is confused in the Folio text of 1623. (The earliest edition, the Quarto of 1600, has virtually no directions here.) That has 'The Governor and some Citizens on the walls' and provides another entry for the Governor before line 44. Editors omit the reference to his appearance at the beginning of the scene and change the direction so that the citizens are found 'on the walls above the gates'. Thus, the real door(s) at the back of the stage would be used for the town gates and the balcony above would serve as the city walls – an identical arrangement to that for Richard II's surrender at Flint Castle in the first play of the tetralogy. Possibly some of the audience might contrast the memory of Richard's 'descent into the base court' to surrender to the usurper, Henry Bolingbroke, Henry V's father, with this scene.

As so often in this play, no success or pleasure comes unalloyed. The victor of Harfleur knows that sickness, the scourge of medieval and renaissance armies, is sweeping through the ranks.

Act III, Scene iv

Summary
Shakespeare now sets before his audience a scene completely different in setting and tone from anything that has gone before. Princess Katharine, daughter of Charles VI of France and his queen, Isobel, is shown being given a lesson in the English language by an old Gentlewoman.

Commentary
On the surface, this is a very simple rehearsal of English equivalents for a few French words for parts of the body. It *seems* delightfully simple, even innocent, and so it was as played by the young Rene Asherson in Olivier's film version. Perhaps no scene in the film is more misleading as to what is really going on and probably most members of audience in the theatre miss the scene's implications for V.ii. Whilst the *surface* impression is one of coy fun, there is something disturbing tucked away in this scene.

Language lessons, or lessons in writing letters, occur within a number of plays at about this time. The tradition is also to be found in French drama and in a number of French farces such lessons end with obscenities similar to that found in *Henry V*. Modern editors set the scene in Rouen, picking up the king's reference at the end of the next scene (64) and where, according to Holinshed and Halle the French court then was. The French is usually modernised and to some extent corrected. Princess Katharine would originally have been played by a boy actor; the old lady-in-waiting was probably played by a man.

The most obvious implication of the scene is that it looks forward to the outcome of the story. Of course, as the first audiences well knew that Henry married Katharine, there was no point in Shakespeare's dramatising this as if it were merely a possibility. As there is no dramatic tension to be derived – will they marry? – Shakespeare makes the scene serve other dramatic ends. Katharine *is* France's fair cities. This is no critical flight of fancy: the precise equation is made in the final scene of the play (see V.ii and 7.9). She *is* 'La Belle France' and the audience can thus see Henry's prize in female and national form.

But what of the language itself? Why choose *these* words? Might not the English for *chambre*, *chaise*, *table*, *fenêtre*, serve the function of a lesson quite as well? The clue to the answer lies in the obscenity implied at the scene's end in *le count*. We must suppose that 'nick' could be understood obscenely – notice how 'chin' is taken as 'sin'. The word 'bilbow' undoubtedly refers to the blisters associated with venereal disease (contrast contemporary herpes), and probably 'foot', pronounced without the final 't', as if it were a French word (compare *bout*), is also intended to be obscene. There is thus a heavy concentration of obscenities at the end of this scene and these stand in striking contrast to its surface innocence. That these words really are as they are described here (and some editions either studiously avoid mentioning this fact, or offer a bland generalised statement, or even downright error) is apparent from the Princess's shocked reaction: these words are 'mauvais, corruptible, gros, et impudique'. She does not say words in the singular, but 'mots'. They are certainly not words that she could repeat before French gentlemen.

Our first impression of Katharine as a closely-guarded, gently-nurtured, sweet innocent must to some extent be qualified; she is not so innocent as knowingly coy. More important will be the recall of this scene at the end of the play. Shakespeare hammers home the obscenity, not to prompt cheap laughter, but to make us remember this moment for later in the play. Unfortunately that later scene is often cut, probably because directors don't understand the point that Shakespeare is making.

Olivier in his film makes the neatest of transitions between this scene and the next by taking up Katharine's last four words, 'allons nous à diner', as she hurries to join the men of the court who are already at table (in III.v). On the way she and her lady see from the battlements the French Herald, Montjoy, returning to the court after bidding farewell to the English message-bearers (Exeter and his train of II.iv). This is not called for by Shakespeare and is not necessary in the theatre, but it makes good filmic sense.

Act III, Scene v

Summary
The French courtiers express their dismay that Henry and his army have gone so far unchallenged. The king orders his nobles to take the field and to bring Henry captive to Rouen, whilst his courtiers stand amazed that those from so 'foggy, raw and dull' (16) a climate can show such valiant spirit.

Commentary
Shakespeare capitalises in an interesting way on the age-old assumption that a people is conditioned by the climate in which it lives. He records the myth but shows it is unfounded. It is the French who are 'raw and dull' and the English who have shown 'quick blood', as if 'spirited with wine'. The contempt of the French for the English forces will contrast strikingly with the overwhelming defeat of the French and, in the twentieth century, was repeated in the German attitude to the 'contemptible little army' sent to France by Britain in 1914. In fact, Henry's army was in a sorry state. It was seriously weakened by illness and was short of basic necessities. It is noticeable that here, even the level-headed Constable pours contempt upon his foes wishing Henry's army were not so weak and small. Thus Shakespeare makes much more of the eventual downfall of those who boast.

Act III, Scene vi

Summary
Henry's army has marched north-east from Harfleur towards Calais and is in Picardy. The scene treats of four matters. First we learn of the Duke of Exeter's great service in securing the bridge (though historically he was not present); second, Pistol's appeal against Bardolph's sentence of death is heard; third, Fluellen reports to the king on the success at the bridge and indirectly and good-heartedly makes an appeal on Bardolph's behalf; finally, the French herald, Montjoy, appears to make a final appeal to Henry that he should not sacrifice his men in what must be a lost cause. Henry, though he treats the herald generously (164), will not surrender.

Commentary

Shakespeare juxtaposes two characters, Fluellen and Pistol, both of whom speak extravagantly. Both are comic, but there is a difference in the ways we respond to them. Fluellen, for all his absurdity, has a touch of that quality he finds in the Duke of Exeter: magnanimity (strainedly punned with Agamemmon). This is something Pistol plainly lacks. But the contrast goes further and in a curiously different direction. For once Pistol seeks to do something for someone else in his attempt to save Bardolph from being hanged. Fluellen, however, is shown to be guilty of quite serious misjudgement of Pistol's character. Gower, who doesn't know Pistol, acutely sums him up some forty lines earlier as 'an arrant counterfeit rascal' (62). Fluellen is taken in by 'prave words' (64).

Bardolph's crime was really committed according to Holinshed (see p.20), though the soldier executed in *Henry V* was guilty of a much less serious offence. Bardolph stole a pax (41), a small metal plate bearing a crucifix; the historical soldier stole a pyx and ate the consecrated bread (representing the body of Christ) which it contained, so hungry was he. Shakespeare greatly lessens the offence and thus makes the punishment, and Henry's 'discipline' (57), which Fluellen so readily accepts, far more extreme. It is worth noting, too, that the death of Bardolph is one of the very few deaths, especially by execution, of a clown in sixteenth- and seventeenth-century drama. The Elizabethan audience could not but reflect that in this play no less than *three* clowns die: Falstaff (off-stage), Bardolph, and Nym (see 7.6).

The 1600 edition of the play has a couple of lines at Pistol's exit that were probably inserted by the actors – 'ad libs'. After Fluellen's 'Very good' in response to Pistol's parting obscenity, Pistol repeats and develops his gibe:

Pistol: I say the fig within thy bowels and thy dirty maw. [*Exit*]
Fluellen: Captain Gower, cannot you hear it lighten and thunder?

The stage direction at Henry's entry contains a telling description which is to be found in the 1623 Folio: 'Enter the King and his poore Souldiers'. Henry's army is in a visibly sorry state and it will need all Henry's spirit and skill to make it an effective fighting force. Despite his support of discipline when he is speaking to Pistol, Fluellen makes an indirect appeal for Bardolph's life: if executed, he will be the only casualty of this hard fight, and he will have died at English, not French, hands. The king's response is so proper, so in line with the decorum of conducting war, that he can seem cold, even pompous. (For Montjoy's contemptuous message from the French king and Henry's reply, see p.61.)

After the herald has gone, there is a brief but poignant exchange between Henry and Gloucester which makes plain the weakness of the English forces and, in contrast, the strength of Henry's faith in God.

Notice that the French herald uses a theatrical image, 'now speak we upon our cue' (128), subtly reminding the audience that it is still only seeing a theatrical representation of these great events.

Act III, Scene vii

Summary and Commentary

In the long hours before the battle, the French nobles are seen in desultory conversation. Shakespeare skilfully dramatises their empty boasting, the dragging time, and the tensions between the characters. The Dauphin, who was not, in fact, present at the battle, and the Constable are characterised as sharply different. The conflict between them is well hit off by the exchange of proverbs (63–9), which concludes with the Constable's icy rebuff of the Dauphin, requiring a quick change in the tenor of the conversation, initiated by Rambures. It is again Rambures who, at the end of the scene, expresses a note of caution:English mastiffs are of unmatchable courage. His caution is given short shrift by Orleans. They are merely 'Foolish curs!'

Act IV, Chorus

Summary

Both armies await morning and the battle. The English are described as 'condemned like sacrifices'; the French as over-confident, playing at dice with each other with English prisoners, yet to be captured, as their stakes. Henry visits his men to assess and build up their spirits. Having drawn a vivid and compelling picture of the night before battle, so ensuring the audience make their 'imaginary forces work', Shakespeare virtually undermines all he has achieved in the last six lines: it is, after all, only a play which presents a famous battle 'in brawl ridiculous' (51).

Commentary

This Chorus is often placed in production before III.vii. Indeed, it may well serve in a modern two-part version of the play as the Chorus which opens the second part of the production, to be followed by III.vii and then IV.i. It is a wonderfully evocative Chorus and movingly conjures up in our minds the atmosphere of the night before a battle between two unevenly matched forces, one facing virtual annihilation. Shakespeare contrasts the technical preparations (the armourers noisily closing up the rivets of armour, the horses neighing) with the natural sounds of the countryside. The winking lights of camp-fires contrast with the image of royalty: the sun.

Shakespeare concentrates on the wretched state of the English soldiers. They are already condemned, yet wait patiently for their fate; they are already 'horrid ghosts' (28). Notice their 'watchful fires' (23). It is not, of course, their fires that keep watch, but it is as if the camp-fires were keeping guard over those who sit about them.

There is no evidence that Henry V visited his men before the Battle of Agincourt but he is reported to have done so during the siege of Harfleur. What might have prompted the scene in Shakespeare's mind was the famous visit Queen Elizabeth made to her forces at Tilbury in 1588 when they were assembled to meet a threatened Spanish invasion should the Armada prove successful. This had made a lasting impression on the public mind and her speech, 'I know I have the body of a weak and feeble woman, but I have the heart and stomach of a king, and a king of England, too', was well-known.

Why, after the unforgettable line, 'A little touch of Harry in the night' (47), Shakespeare should have so undercut the atmosphere he had created by ridiculing his company's production is difficult to explain. The effect anticipates Brecht's technique of alienation by nearly four centuries. It is not a risk most modern producers will take and these last six lines of the Chorus are usually cut.

Act IV, Scene i

Summary
On the eve of the battle, Henry is dramatised in a sequence of relationships: with his nobles, with Pistol, overhearing two of his captains, Fluellen and Gower, and then, most lengthily, in a debate with three private soldiers on the morality of war. When the soldiers leave the stage to Henry, he ponders first on the implications of what they have said to him, and then on the nature of kingship. He is briefly interrupted by Sir Thomas Erpingham, anxious because Henry has been absent for so long. The scene closes (apart from Gloucester's call to the king) with Henry's prayer that God will favour his cause. Central to that prayer is Henry's plea that his father's usurpation of Richard II's throne be overlooked. Henry promises further endowments in benefit of Richard's soul.

Commentary
This is a remarkable scene, perhaps one of the most remarkable in all

Shakespeare. There are finer speeches, moments of greater tension, poetry of greater beauty, elsewhere in Shakespeare's plays, but nowhere else does Shakespeare so strikingly and effectively seek to come to terms with the dilemmas attendant upon ruling and being ruled. In his dramatisation of this confrontation of king and commoner, commander and private, and in the frankness of their exchange, Shakespeare is doing something very unusual. There was a tradition that leaders visited their men at night, but, in practice, the ordinary soldier is far removed from the high command. We can still, in our more democratic age, get some impression of the novelty and force of Henry's visitation of his men and the boldness of the soldiers' attitudes, from events in this century. In the 1939–45 War, Generals Wingate and Montgomery were remarkable for the extent to which they met and talked to their men. Barrie Pitt, writing in *1918: The Last Act* (Macmillan, 1984 edn, p.18) says:

> Only one army commander seems to have made regular inspections of conditions at the front, and after 1914, no one in the higher ranks ever spent as long as one week living the life of the front line infantry in the trenches.

The boldness of Shakespeare's conception is thus still remarkable in this century.

The scene is also remarkable for the skill with which Shakespeare contrasts Henry's confrontations with the different elements of his army. He begins by seeming almost to admonish Gloucester for suggesting that so steadfast a leader as Erpingham, however aged, would be better at home in bed. The little scene with Pistol is both comic for Pistol's lack of reverence and ironically complimentary to Henry: 'The king's a bawcock, and a heart of gold' (44). There is also a neat contrast between Pistol's bombast and the direct simplicity of Williams that follows.

It is the discussion with the soldiers that is the centrepiece of the scene, even of the play. In the film, where the sound system permits of much quieter speech than that practical in a large theatre, a peculiar degree of intimacy was built up. It is noticeable how fluently Williams argues. It is no accident that Shakespeare gives him a Welsh name (and Henry has just claimed to Pistol that he, too, is Welsh, and what is more, Fluellen's kinsman, 51 and 59). It is surely astonishing that Shakespeare could have so openly and strongly dramatised the questioning of military leadership – of authority – in a society in which concern for order and the duty of obedience were so important (see 2.3). Of course, Williams will fight, and we may

presume valiantly, and he will be rewarded with a purse of money by
the king, but he has made his points and Henry does not – perhaps
cannot – answer them all. Two of Williams's points are especially
telling. 'If the cause be not good, the king himself hath a heavy
reckoning to make' (135), he says, and he goes on to speak of those
who die not well in battle. The king only answers the latter part of
Williams's argument directly, maintaining, quite properly, that a
man's sins must be upon his own head. What he does not take up here
is the matter of the honesty or otherwise of the royal cause if
obedience is to be enjoined on all the king's subjects (but see 6.2,
especially pp.62–4). The 'honesty of royal commands' was to be a
matter of concern in later drama (and, of course, in civil life). Thus,
just over a decade later, Beaumont and Fletcher in *Philaster* have this
exchange between a courtier and a king who demands more than his
authority can ensure:

King: What! Am I not your king?
　　　If aye, then am I not to be obeyed?
Dion: Yes, if you command things possible and honest.
King: Things possible and honest! Hear me, thou,
　　　Thou traitor, that darest confine thy king to things
　　　Possible and honest!　　　　　　　　　　(IV.ii.117–22)

Williams is also sharp enough to see that whereas private soldiers
taken prisoner will have their throats cut, the king, if captured, will
be ransomed. That of course is pretty well what does happen, though
it is the French prisoners, not the English who get their throats
cut – at Henry's instruction (see below, p.44)
　On the surface, Henry seems in his soliloquy simply to be
bemoaning the lot of a king as compared to that of a private
individual, but there is something much more serious at issue here.
What does a king possess that ordinary men and women lack?
Ceremony, he answers himself. And ceremony? It is but an idol,
powerless, worthless, a proud dream. Put very crudely – and it is
essential to stress how crude is this equation – a king = a man +
worthless ceremony. A king, therefore, *is* but a man. Shakespeare
takes further the distinction between man-as-man and man-as-king
that he dramatised in *Richard II* (see *Richard II*, IV.i.203–220, where
Richard 'undoes himself', washing away 'ceremony', until he can
describe himself as 'unkinged' – see 5.4). In this, Shakespeare's plays
are well ahead of that large number that will later take up one aspect
or another of this issue, an issue to be settled in real life by the

execution of Charles I half a century after *Henry V* was written. (See section 6.2 for an analysis of king's meditation.)

Act IV, Scene ii

Summary and Commentary
The long night is over and at first light the French nobles are eager to mount their horses and take to the battlefield. They are still contemptuous of their English foes and the Dauphin ironically suggests giving the starving English soldiers and their horses a good meal before the battle starts. The scene ends with the Constable calling them all to battle as if to a day's hunting. The short scene begins with the sun's first rays striking the French lords' armour and ends with the sun high in the sky and the day already wasting away in inaction. So does Shakespeare give an impression of the rapid passage of events.

Act IV, Scene iii

Summary
This scene is set in contrast to IV.ii. Whereas the French go joyfully to a seemingly certain victory, the English face defeat and death. However, as Westmoreland wishes for men fresh from England, he is interrupted by Henry, whose speech parallels that before Harfleur. Now, instead of rallying his troops for a final effort, he must somehow convince his men that a famous victory is within their grasp. Far from there being too few of them, he says faint hearts can be spared and given money to see them on their way. Montjoy, the French herald, makes one more appeal to Henry to surrender. Henry rejects his proposal and rebukes the herald for mocking the condition of his men. As the herald leaves, the Duke of York begs to lead the advance guard.

Commentary
Shakespeare's audiences knew well the result of Agincourt: it was a victory of legendary standing. His task, therefore, is to stress the unequal nature of the contest, not simply so that the English might boast as chauvinistically as the French nobles, but to enable his audiences to experience anew the achievement of their forbears.

York's part in the play is tiny. This is his only speech. Often in productions these lines will be given to another character – Bedford, for example. This is a pity for Shakespeare is making a small but telling point. The Duke of York is the Aumerle of *Richard II* whom Henry V's father pardoned when he might have been executed for treason. He will prove to be one of the few English casualties of the battle (but see IV, viii). Negotiations between the French and the English were not as they are represented in this scene. In fact, Henry offered to pay for the damage his troops had caused and to forgo some of his claims on France if the French would allow his army safe passage to Calais. He was thus anxious to avoid a battle, so wretched was the state of his army.

Act IV, Scenes iv, v, and vi

Preliminary Note
These battle scenes have two different orders in the texts published in Shakespeare's own day. In the Quarto of 1600, the scene in which the French nobles reproach themselves because the enemy they so despised has the upper hand comes before that between Pistol and M. le Fer; in the Folio of 1623 they are the other way about (and so in most modern editions). This complicates matters because Henry seems to give twice the order that the French prisoners be killed. The order of events (and their repetition) in Holinshed is:

1. The English have taken many prisoners.
2. Some 600 French cavalry, learning that the English camp is unguarded, ravage it and kill the baggage-boys.
3. Henry fearing that the enemy in his midst might mount a new attack and be assisted in this by the many prisoners taken, ordered that all the prisoners be killed. [In ordering this action Henry was following the code of conduct of war as understood in the Renaissance.]
4. The king sees another group of French and sends a herald to them to tell them to fight or quit the field. Failing that, he will order that the throats of the French prisoners – those already taken and those yet to be captured – be cut. The French flee. It will be noted that even in the source, the king twice orders the killing of the prisoners.

Summary
The Dauphin and nobles have been taken by surprise by the stubborn resistance of the English and are filled with shame, but, not lacking courage themselves are prepared to fight to the death. In another part of the field, Pistol is taking M. le Fer prisoner. He is far more concerned with what he can get by ransom than with honour (see 7.7). When he has led away his prisoner, the Boy – just as before Harfleur (III.ii) – soliloquises on what he (and we) have just witnessed and leaves us in no doubt as to Pistol's hollowness. He also reveals to the audience the danger in which the baggage boys are placed.

The third short scene shifts attention to the king. He cautions against assuming victory has already been won. Quite suddenly, interpreting an alarm as the reinforcement of the French forces, he orders the killing of all French prisoners, releasing their captors to fight the French.

Commentary

A battlefield is inevitably confused and it is difficult to see it *in toto*. Still less is it practicable to show it convincingly on the stage. Shakespeare adopts a 'cameo technique'. He dramatises brief moments, none of which shows pitched battles but rather the *effects* of battle. This works well, but the confusion of battle is compounded by confusion in the plotting. Although Holinshed, Shakespeare's source, repeats the order for the killing of the prisoners, his account of the battle is clearer than Shakespeare's. It is necessary to ask whether Shakespeare is himself confused, or whether he is trying to highlight Henry's order to kill the prisoners. There is, even if it were regarded as permissible according to renaissance canons of war, a great difference between killing prisoners because of a supposed reinforcement of the enemy, and after the baggage boys have been murdered. Is Henry being shown as vengeful, or are we being shown the inevitable cruelty of war? (see 7.7)

Pistol is well described by the Boy as but a clown. The traditional theatrical clown was armed with a wooden dagger, with which at the end of the play, he would be beaten away. Like a parasite, he battens on those nobler but less fortunate than himself, just as Falstaff does with Colevile of the Dale at the Battle of Gaultree Forest in *2 Henry IV*, IV. iii. The humour, mainly bawdy, is associated with the dishonourable, with the rotten underbelly of this 'famous victory'.

Act IV, Scene vii

Summary

In sharp contrast to the last lines of the preceding scene, IV. viii starts with Fluellen's announcement that the baggage boys have been killed. Fluellen, in a sequence of speeches, draws a complicated comparison between Henry's virtues and those of Alexander. There is a brief reminiscence of Sir John Falstaff and then the king enters. His speech on the murder of the baggage boys is full of bitter, cold, but tightly controlled anger, giving way to his threat of vengeance. The French herald enters, now much humbled, and begs permission for the French to bury their dead. The battle is named after the neighbouring castle (whose master, Isambert, was one of those who reportedly sacked the baggage train, although Shakespeare does not mention this). Henry meets Williams, with whom he had argued on the eve of the battle. By a subterfuge, Henry sets up Fluellen to take his part in his wager with Williams.

Commentary

Fluellen's opening speech epitomises the complex range of tones that marks this scene. It combines an announcement of a cruel and cowardly killing by armoured knights on unarmed boys, with low comedy. There is the comedy of accent (other people's accents being, so often, a basic ingredient of comedy, especially to the English – see 7.5); the comedy of absurd understatement – it is 'as arrant a piece of knavery'; the appeal to 'the etiquette of war', as if it were a kind of polite convention; and, above all, the ridiculous conjunction of the killing of the boys and the baggage: baggage, of course, is not killed. Fluellen elaborates these absurdities by drawing fantastical comparisons between Henry and Alexander the Great. And all this set against a cruel killing.

Having built up the ridiculous, Shakespeare swiftly shifts the tone to dramatise Henry's anger at the killing of the boys. Usually a soldier, or even Henry, is seen carrying one of the boys, quite possibly identifiable as the Boy who accompanied the trio of clowns to France. The one sane, wholesome spirit of that group has joined the villainous Bardolph in death. The waste of battle is thus graphically dramatised without any need to litter the stage with 'dead' actors.

The setting up by Henry of Williams and Fluellen is a rather pedestrian joke. It looks back to the king's attempt to fool the Drawer in *1 Henry IV*, a game that struck Hal's companion, Poins, as singularly pointless. There is no need for a dramatist to make the characters of different parts of a tetralogy wholly consistent, but it is interesting that Shakespeare seems to make a point of looking back over the earlier plays of the sequence. Of all the things that Henry, as prince and king, found difficult to learn, a sense of humour proved the most elusive.

Act IV, Scene viii

Summary

Comedy and death are again juxtaposed. In the first part of the scene, the wager between Williams and the king, and Henry's joke, come to a head. Williams is rewarded by the king, and, though a shilling seems little to us – 5p – it was at least one-tenth of a week's wages for a skilled craftsman when this play was first performed. Fluellen is genuinely magnanimous and his action should not be

ridiculed in production or criticism. It is now the turn of the English
herald and he recounts the enormous contrast between the French
and English losses. Among the English dead is that Aumerle, now
Edward, Duke of York, who remained loyal to the deposed Richard
II and was taken by Henry IV to be a traitor but pardoned. The scene
closes with Henry's pious thanks to God for the victory.

Commentary

What is so intriguing about Shakespeare's characterization of
Williams, the ordinary soldier, is the marvellous natural dignity and
wealth of commonsense he invests in him. It is given to this character
to provide a gloss to Henry's soliloquy on ceremony (IV.i.242–90):
'what have kings that privates have not too, / Save ceremony?' (244–5)
with his 'you appeared to me but as a commond man' (52). Here
Williams – Shakespeare – really gets to the heart of the matter.
Without your 'ceremony', your trappings of office, you are but as any
other man, says Williams; and has not Henry himself questioned 'idol
ceremony'?

   The figures of casualties exaggerate the difference, as such figures
commonly do. Nevertheless, they were remarkably different. There
were probably some 7000 French casualties and 400 –500 English.
This exaggeration is not Shakespeare's but his sources'. For the
religious thanksgiving, Shakespeare also follows his sources. One
little irony. York's death was not particularly glorious. He fell from
his horse and died either from suffocation or a heart attack.

Act V, Chorus

Summary and Commentary

This is the least memorable of the Choruses and in production is
often savagely cut. It summarises the events of the five years between
Agincourt and the Treaty of Troyes. Henry and his army returned to
England after their victory; later, Sigismund, the Holy Roman
Emperor, visited England to plead the French cause. Henry then
returned to France for the final settlement of Troyes. His second
campaign is ignored in this telescoping of events and it often seems to
an audience that what now is dramatised follows on directly after the
Battle of Agincourt. Olivier, in his film, at least stressed a difference
in season. Agincourt took place in the month of October and Fluellen
here refers to St David's Day, 1 March. Thus the snowy landscape of
the film gave an impression of some shift in time.

Act V, Scene i

Summary
Pistol is finally put down. His military qualities are shown to be mere bluster. Fluellen forces him to eat the leek he so despised and he is rebuked by Gower. As when representing the king in the confrontation with Williams, Fluellen again shows his generosity of spirit, even to one such as Pistol. Pistol concludes the scene with a sour little monologue in which he plans his future deception when he is back in England and takes on the imposture of an old and worthy soldier.

Commentary
Although it is four years later, the paralleling of the Fluellen –Williams and the Fluellen–Pistol confrontations suggests continuity of action. Thus, for those who listen, the passage of time is made plain, but the bittiness of the old pageant-like chronicle play is artistically avoided. For the purposes of drama – for the work of art – Henry's courtship of the Princess of France will seem a logical outcome of the victory of Agincourt and thus can Shakespeare achieve an aesthetic unity. Further, the union of Henry and Katharine, though blatantly a political contrivance, can be tinged with romance, and its short-lived nature glossed over. That will be another story.

Pistol's final speech is curiously out of character. There are fairly strong grounds for suggesting that it was originally intended for Falstaff, who could certainly claim 'Old do I wax', the reference to Honour being cudgelled from his limbs glancing back to his famous speech on the emptiness of Honour in *I Henry IV* (V.i. 130–40). Even more telling is the name, Doll, which appears in the early texts. Doll was Falstaff's 'meat' (*2 Henry IV*, II.iv.121). Earlier in *Henry V* Pistol has told Nym to find Doll in the hospital where she is lying, suffering from venereal disease, and, he says, he will have and hold 'the quondam Quickly / For the only she', implying by 'have and hold' (from the marriage ceremony) his intention to wed her (II.i.74–9). It is usual in productions to change 'Doll' to 'Nell', but the texts do suggest that Falstaff did once figure in this play and that revision has not been quite thorough.

Act V, Scene ii

Summary
The last scene of the play is one of reconciliation. The events dramatised took place in 1420, five years after Agincourt. This reconciliation is, in the first place, political. It is engineered by the Duke of Burgundy who, in 1419, sided with the English after the murder of his father by the Dauphin. He describes his role in lines

24–28. The political settlement was marked by the Treaty of Troyes (glanced at, 75–83) and then sealed by the betrothal of Katharine and Henry. Henry's wooing of Katharine has, on the surface, all the appearance of the conclusion to a comedy. In this it may be contrasted with, say, Rosalind and Orlando in *As You Like It* and her teaching him to woo. However, this 'happy end' is qualified quite seriously by the manner of Henry's wooing, by Burgundy's rebuke, 'pardon the frankness of my mirth' (309), and by Henry's language in which he describes his 'conquest' of Kate.

Commentary

Perhaps Shakespeare's most remarkable structural skill was his ability to bring a play to a satisfying aesthetic conclusion yet to point simultaneously to its less comfortable aspects. Thus *As You Like It* is rounded off not with one but with four weddings. Yet, if we think at all, we must ask which of these is victualled for more than a month, or, for the couple proposing to live in the forest, for even as long as that. *Henry V* ends 'like a comedy'. All seems to be concluded neatly and happily, at least for the English. They have won a glorious victory – genuine enough; the French, to the audience an ancient enemy, have been satisfactorily humiliated; peace and its virtues are extolled by Burgundy in a beautifully judged speech; a Treaty is agreed; a betrothal made; and all is well in the gardens of England and France. Or is it?

Now it is most important in reading what follows to continue to accept that at one level of our apprehension this 'happy end' remains true. In effect, Shakespeare has his cake and eats it – a trick, or feat, of art that marks his genius and gives the ending of this play a special strength far removed from the crude chauvinism some people will find in this play.

Take, for example, Burgundy, the fine speech-maker and, seemingly, the peacemaker. The well-informed of Shakespeare's first audience would be aware that Burgundy was, to the French, a traitor. Even though national identity in early fifteenth-century France was not, perhaps, quite so strongly defined as it has become, there was no getting away from the fact that disputes within the French parties led to Burgundy's siding with Henry. He speaks, therefore, not as an independent arbiter but as an interested participant. It is simply not correct to argue, as does Sally Beauman justifying giving these lines to Chorus in the 1975 RSC production, that it doesn't matter who speaks them. Shakespeare's cunning may be too much for a twentieth-century audience but it should not escape the comprehension of the Royal Shakespeare Company.

There is, too, irony in the wooing scene. There was, and still is, a tradition in low and high comedy of 'teaching the clown to woo'. In low comedy, the clown is just that: a Fool or one of such a pair as Morecambe and Wise. In high comedy the person to be taught may be made foolish by love, like Orlando in *As You Like It*, taught to woo by Rosalind dressed as a man. Here a king, claiming to be but a tongue-tied soldier – king as common man again – begs to be taught how to 'plead his love-suit' (101). But, ironically, he hardly needs teaching: he never stops talking. This is hardly wooing but rather a verbal assault upon Katharine, in the manner of Henry's assaults upon the French towns and cities to which Katharine is to be likened later in the scene (336–47).

Looking a little further ahead, it cannot be denied that Henry's victory at Agincourt, spectacular though it undoubtedly was, was short-lived. Two years after the Treaty of Troyes, which we now see being agreed, Henry V died of dysentery. All he had fought for would be lost and England would go through a turbulent century, particularly under the son born to him and Katharine, Henry VI. To some degree that would be balanced in the minds of Shakespeare's better-informed audiences because Katharine's grandson by her second husband, Owen Tudor, would be crowned Henry VII, inaugurating the line of Tudor monarchs. Elizabeth I was the great-great-granddaughter of Katharine of France (but not of Henry V).

However, the most telling aspect of the scene is one too often ignored, cut from productions, or at best, glossed over in footnotes to scholarly editions (e.g. the New Arden). It was cut from Olivier's film and from the Royal Shakespeare Company's 400th Anniversary production of 1964 and their 1975 production. This begins with Burgundy seeking pardon for 'the frankness of his mirth', continues with the obsessive play made on such words as *con*jure, picking up Katharine's shock earlier in the play at words 'mauvais, corruptible, gros et impudique' at the end of her language lesson (III.iv. 33–4, and see p.36 above), and it concludes with Kate's being likened to a French city that Henry has assaulted: 'the cities turned into a maid . . . the maid that stood in the way' (339, 345–6). Notice too how Kate is numbered among those maids who, 'well summered', become like flies, blind (=lustful) and 'then they will endure handling' (325–8).

In these ways, Shakespeare ensures that the overall 'comedic' tone of the ending is sustained but that, if we listen and think, we can tell that, as with the comedy throughout the play, there is a sour note to this celebration.

Final Chorus

Summary and Commentary

After the exuberance of his earlier speeches. Chorus ends on a somewhat subdued note, reflecting the ambivalent tone of what has gone just before. His speech takes the form of a sonnet – a love poem often enough at this time – but having recorded Henry's achievement in gaining 'the world's best garden' (looking back to Gaunt's description in *Richard II*: 'This other Eden . . . This blessed plot', and the Under-Gardener's reference to 'our sea-walled garden', II.i.42, 50 and III.iv. 43), he points to what will follow: the loss of France and bloodshed in England, a story often replayed by Shakespeare's own company, not least in his three parts of *Henry VI* and in *Richard III*.

5 THEMES AND ISSUES

5.1 LESSONS TO BE LEARNED

There is a danger that we read great literature to extract lessons from it as if authors were preachers and their readers wayward members of their flocks. It would be strange in writing that describes or dramatises a life we can recognise if there were not something to be discovered that enlightened or inspired us; but teaching lessons as such is not a function of art and extracting morals from books like plums out of a pudding is to be deplored. Great art is more finely balanced and less obvious in its assessments than is reducible to simple moralising. Often the ambiguities and uncertainties call for judgements from us and that will mean that individuals will come to different conclusions. Thus, it would be quite wrong to draw a lesson from *Henry V* that 'a just cause vigorously pursued will be crowned with success'; seven years later, Henry, still pursuing what he took to be a rightful cause, was dead of dysentery and, as the final Chorus indicates, England lapsed into internecine strife.

In the light of this caution it is slightly paradoxical to point to the attention given to lessons to be learned in this play, and, indeed, in the whole tetralogy. There is an overall concern with 'the education of a prince' in *1* and *2 Henry IV*, and in *Henry V* there is a formal lesson (Katharine's English lesson) and a plea by Henry to be taught the language of love. Canterbury, in the play's first scene, harps upon the able scholar Henry has become: 'Never was such a sudden scholar made' (32); his learning is now such he might qualify as a prelate (40); he can so debate the issues of state, you would think he had devoted his whole life to their examination (41–2), and so on. Not only is Henry now, it seems, a scholar, but the Dauphin is also to be lessoned: 'We'll chide the Dauphin at his father's door', says the king (I.ii.308).

In II.ii, an ironic lesson is played out. Henry declines the advice of Scroop, Cambridge, and Grey and releases the drunken railer, and then the king treats them to the advice they had given him. A bitter lesson indeed.

More obvious lessons are Kate's English lesson and that taught Pistol. As Gower puts it, 'let a Welsh correction teach you a good English condition' (V.i.82–3). There is probably also a lesson in the advantages of unity demonstrated by the need for Fluellen, Gower, Jamy, and Macmorris to work together. Power can only derive from a union of the parts and that union should conclude dissensions between ancient rivalries. It is noticeable that British success comes at the expense of a French Court riven by dissension.

The most interesting pupil, however, is Henry. Despite his long apprenticeship, and 'Consideration' 'whipped the offending Adam out of him' (I.i.28–9) – an echo of the Anglican service of baptism, as if the king were again new-born – he has not completed the process of learning. His confrontation with Williams is a kind of schooling and it is a lesson which he seems to take to heart.

What of the play's last lesson, in wooing? Henry begins by asking to be taught 'terms / Such as will enter at a lady's ear' (V.ii.99–100). That part of the scene concludes with his teaching her that 'nice customs curtsy to great kings' (284). When the Court re-enters, Burgundy asks if Henry has been teaching the Princess English and Henry replies that the only lesson he is trying to impart is 'how perfectly I love her' (298–301). The stress on learning is apparent. It has to be asked, however, whether Henry really has learned to the full the lessons drawn from the invasion of France. As has been suggested in the Commentary (and see 7.9), Kate is likened to a French city and Henry, in effect, assaults her verbally by non-stop wooing, rather as he has physically assaulted the cities of France. Although he pays her courtesies – 'You have witchcraft in your lips, Kate; there is more eloquence in a sugar touch of them than in the tongues of the French council' (292–4) – he treats her before the Court as no better than a thing to be subjected to his will (345–7). Henry still has lessons to learn. Note, too, how Burgundy's crude reference to maids 'enduring handling' (328) is taken further by Henry. When the Hostess reluctantly admits, yes, Falstaff 'did in some sort, indeed, handle women' (II.iii.38), she offers an excuse, though it hardly redeems him: 'but then he was rheumatic, and talked of the whore of Babylon' (38–40). Does Shakespeare expect us to draw a parallel?

It does not seem beyond the bounds of directorial ingenuity to get across to an audience the purport of this part of the final scene (from

Burgundy's 'Pardon the frankness of my mirth', 309). Yet it is invariably savagely cut – so in Olivier's film; so in the 1964 400th Anniversary Royal Shakespeare production; and the RSC 1975 production to mark the centenary of the Stratford Memorial Theatre, 'after more than four months of preparation and rehearsal', cut *everything* from Burgundy's speech at the re-entry of the Court (298) to the French king's, 'We have consented to all terms of reason' (348). The reason? Terry Hands, Director of the 1975 production explains:

> the cuts here were forced upon us by the audience; the marriage has been agreed; soon we will all of us want to go home. And the rest of the scene, which is important, is held up by these courtly circumlocutions. (B.228)

We all want to go home! Such, alas, is the level of apprehension of our premier Shakespeare company! Despite the opening paragraph to this section, perhaps there are lessons to be learned from Shakespeare's *Henry V*: learning is a continuous process.

5.2   THE EXERCISE OF AUTHORITY

There is in *Hamlet* a well-known passage that sums up one attitude to the monarch at the end of the sixteenth century:

> There's such divinity doth hedge a king
> That treason can but peep to what it would,
> Acts little of his will. (IV.v.124–6)

It seems to imply divine protection for the monarch but it must not be read out of context. It is said by Claudius, a usurper, who is killed at the end of the play and who reached the throne as a result of the assassination of Hamlet's father. Treason seems free to act despite Claudius's confidence in divine protection.

This passage exemplifies Shakespeare's interest in this topic. This does not mean he is 'writing about' the nature of authority. It arises, in part, as a natural result of something that is at issue in many of his plays as a result of the dramatic action: the exercise of authority. This does not apply solely to the history plays. It is true also of some of the comedies. Thus, even the powers of a fairy-king are at issue in *A Midsummer Night's Dream*, and in *The Tempest* an authority invested with 'white magic' is dramatised.

5.3 THE DIVINE RIGHT OF KINGS

Shakespeare also reflects in some of his plays something that had come to the fore at the end of the sixteenth century: the Divine Right of Kings. In the time of Richard II, this was natural rather than theoretical. Thus, in the poem written in his reign, *Piers Plowman*, an angel from heaven speaks of a king as, 'O qui iura regis. Christi specialia regis' – 'O thou who administers the special law of Christ the King'; a little later the common people cry (also in Latin), 'The precepts of the king are to us the bonds of law'. Historical perspective came in only slowly in the sixteenth century, following considerably after perspective was introduced into painting, and Shakespeare invokes in *Richard II* a theoretical interpretation of Divine Right drawn from his own day, two centuries after the events dramatised.

The theory of Divine Right began to have particular relevance in England after Henry VIII broke with Rome and assumed Headship of the Church of England as well as being Head of the State. Queen Elizabeth I was hardly a monarch to brook limitations to her role as monarch but she chose her ministers well and handled Parliament with skill and tact, so the issue of Divine Right was not contentious. However, at the time *Henry V* was being performed, James VI of Scotland, soon to become James I of England, was writing books and making speeches (published in 1616 in his collected words) which in no uncertain terms outlined the theory of Divine Right and showed how he intended to put it into effect. It was this that was 'in the air' at the end of Elizabeth's reign and which became so dominant in politics after James's accession that, not surprisingly, it was frequently reflected by many dramatists in their plays. According to James:

> Kings are justly called Gods, for that they exercise a manner or resemblance of Divine power upon earth. For if you will consider the attributes to God, you shall see how they agree in the person of a king . . . they have power of raising and casting down; of life and of death; judges over all their subjects and in all causes, and yet accountable to none but God only.

This last claim, that the king was not accountable to the people, proved difficult for Parliament to accept. It was agreed by Parliament and king that there was a 'mutual paction . . . between the king and his people' which the king confirmed at his coronation (and which, indeed, monarchs still do in Britain). However, Parliament claimed that if the king did not keep his part of the contract, the people (=

Parliament) were released from their part of this bargain – as in the terms of ordinary contract law to this day. This James could not accept. *His* contract, he said, was made with God and if he broke his part of the bargain, that was a matter for God; the people were still bound to obey him:

> God must first give sentence upon the king that breaketh,
> before the people can think themselves freed of their oath.

Compare this with the lines Shakespeare gives John of Gaunt in *Richard II* when the Duchess of Gloucester seeks revenge on Richard for her husband's murder:

> God's is the quarrel – for God's substitute
> His deputy anointed in His sight,
> Hath caused the death [of Gloucester]; the which if wrongfully,
> Let heaven revenge, for I may never lift
> An angry arm against His minister. (I.ii.37—41)

On another occasion James argued 'it is presumption and high contempt in a subject to dispute what a king can do, or say that a king cannot do this or that'. Further, almost like a petulant child, he maintained no one might 'meddle with the main points of government; that is my craft . . . I must not be taught my office'.

5.4 DRAMATISING POLITICAL ISSUES

James was making explicit (and hardening) what was understood less formally on this matter at the time Shakespeare was writing the second tetralogy. It is against that background that Richard II's deposition, Private Williams's argument with Henry V, and Henry's own meditation on ceremony need to be read. Some critics seem to conceive of Shakespeare as a very cautious writer, claiming that he too–closely mirrors 'establishment' attitudes. His gifts as a poet, as a creator and innovator of language, have never been disputed, but it is often suggested that he was traditional in dramatic technique and in his thematic materials. I take a different view. I find Shakespeare bolder in his handling of sensitive political matters and far more innovative in the theatre than his contemporaries. What may cause us to think otherwise is the skill with which he handles sensitive issues. Ben Jonson and Thomas Nashe could set London by the ears with their slanderous satire, *The Isle of Dogs* in 1597 with the result that three actors (including Jonson) went to prison and all the theatres were closed down (at first, it was feared, for all time). In that sense Shakespeare was cautious. What he did achieve, however, was far more long-lasting, and, in its own day, much more telling, than a nine-day wonder such as *The Isle of Dogs* scandal: he dramatised the detailed deposition of a monarch and a debate on the nature of kingship.

5.5 THE KING'S TWO BODIES

Central to this debate was a concept of the duality of the person of the monarch. This is known as the theory of the King's Two Bodies. The topic may have worn out its welcome since E. H. Kantorowicz wrote about this in 1957, but it does explain much that is significant to *Richard II* and *Henry V*. Put simply, it is argued that a king has two aspects, one is divine and the other is human. As God's anointed, these were not properly separable. Thus the king's two bodies.

Shakespeare dramatises the 'unkinging' of Richard (and Shakespeare creates the word 'unkinged' for the process of Richard's 'undoing' himself – *Richard II*, IV.i.203 and 220). Richard says only he can perform this office, because only God's deputy can depose an anointed king. He gives up the crown and sceptre (the physical objects of kingship), and then

> With mine own tears I wash away my balm,
> With mine own hands I give away my crown,
> With mine own tongue deny my sacred state,
> With mine own breath release all duteous oaths;
> All pomp and majesty I do forswear;
> My manors, rents, revenues, I forgo;
> My acts, decrees, and statutes I deny. (IV.i.207–13)

In other words, he removes from himself, or washes away, all 'ceremony'. If this is contrasted with Henry V's meditation on ceremony, it will be seen that several of the same images recur – the crown, sceptre, balm, and even rents. In both plays, the later looking back to the earlier, Shakespeare is dramatising one of the most sensitive issues of his time. In doing so he paved the way for many later and lesser dramatists who took up this issue. What is more, in *Henry V*, he goes over the ground three times. Prior to this soliloquy he explained to the soldiers:

> I think the king is but a man, as I am. The violet smells to him as it doth to me; the element shows to him as it doth to me; all his senses

have but human conditions; his ceremonies laid by, in his naked-
ness he appears but a man; and though his affections are higher
mounted than ours, yet when they stoop, they stoop with the like
wing. (108–8)

Note the ambiguity of 'I think the king is but a man, *as I am*'. Then,
after Agincourt, Williams will defend himself with

Your majesty came not like yourself: you appeared to me but as a
common man (51–2)

What Shakespeare dramatises in *Richard II* and *Henry V* is the
twin characteristics of these kings, 'twin-born with greatness'
(IV.i.240): the divine and the human, and the fact that even a rightful
monarch might be deposed. It is no wonder that Queen Elizabeth I
was troubled by performances of *Richard II*, so much so that she
could tell her Keeper of Records, 'I am Richard II, know ye not
that?' It was not until 1608, after James had been established on the
throne for five years and had survived the Gunpowder Plot, that the
deposition scene in *Richard II* was permitted to be printed, and only
then in a greatly shortened form. This matter was political dynamite.
In time the issue of 'the king's two bodies' was to be resolved
symbolically and physically by the separation of the head from the
body of James's son, Charles I (ironically illustrated at the time in a
print titled The Tragic Theatre).

Although the niceties of Divine Right and the King's Two Bodies
are no longer our direct concern, so much so that they have to be
explained at some length, they still subconsciously inform authority
and the way it is exercised. On the one hand, people may not claim
Divine Right, but they may act as if they had God-given powers; on
the other, the disorders attendant upon the failure of central authority are as prevalent now as they were in Shakespeare's time. How we
reconcile the contrasting claims of authority, order, and individual
liberty, nationally and internationally, are no nearer being solved
than when Shakespeare wrote *Richard II* and *Henry V*.

6 TECHNICAL FEATURES

6.1 VARIETIES OF LANGUAGE IN *HENRY V*

At its simplest, the language of *Henry V* is of three kinds: prose,
blank and rhymed verse. About 57 per cent of the play is in blank
verse, 40 per cent in prose and just 3 per cent in rhyme. Blank verse is
composed of ten-syllable lines made up of alternating unstressed and
stressed syllables, each pair being known as an 'iamb', five of which go
to a regular line (hence the technical term, 'iambic pentameter'):
'Once móre untó the breách, dear friénds, once móre'. The first task
of the dramatic poet is to ensure that stress falls on more rather than
less significant syllables so that rhythm enforces meaning. Blank
verse is sometimes said to be the 'natural' verse form for the English
language. Whilst we don't speak or write in blank verse, it is
surprising how closely on occasion Shakespeare is able to adapt the
prose of his source materials to produce verse in this form. He even
jokes about speaking blank verse in ordinary conversation (in *As You
Like It*, IV.i.29). If it is relatively easy to cast a line of blank verse,
doing so with variety and subtly demands art. Too much regularity,
and a lack of variation in the placing of the half-pause (the caesura)
that falls about the middle of most lines, quickly becomes tedious.
There must be a tension between the set, expected pattern of rhythm
and stress and a variation therefrom that 'tricks expectancy' without
shattering the metric effect – and which supports the sense. Look,
for example, at the irregular line, 'Rather proclaim it, Westmoreland, through my host' (IV.iii.34) and note how the stress on the first
two syllables is inverted: Ráther; how the line has 'too many
syllables' (is 'hypermetric'); then, having recorded these mechanical
details, consider their effect and their relationship to what is being
said. By so placing 'Rather' that it alters the position of the expected
stress for the line (and he could easily have made the line regular at

this point by starting, 'But rather'), Shakespeare subtly heightens the contrast of Henry's action with Westmoreland's wish. Then the run of unstressed syllables making up Westmoreland's name seems to imply a stress on each succeeding monosyllable: 'Ráther proclaím it, Westmoreland, through my host'. And the caesura? Is there one? None? Two? Contrast this line with that immediately preceding it where a pause is firmly placed after 'have'. In these ways, metre is not only varied but it helps dramatise the sense.

Quite commonly Shakespeare will close a scene, or even a speech, with a rhyming couplet (e.g. I.i, I.ii, and II.ii, but not the prose scene, II.i, nor II.iv). This serves as a kind of punctuation, drawing events to a temporary close and especially useful in a theatre without a front-of-stage curtain. Note the almost-rhyme that concludes the king's speech at the beginning of III.i: charge/George.

Shakespeare's plays tend to have individual characteristics which are in part determined by his choice, conscious or unconscious, of dominating images. Thus, in *Antony and Cleopatra* the 'worlds' of Egypt and Rome are 'visualised' contrastingly so that Egypt is soft, languorous, luxurious and diseased, whilst the images chosen to represent Rome are metallic, harsh, disciplined and upright. Henry V, unsurprisingly, is likened to the sun directly (Chorus IV, 43) and indirectly as at I.ii.278–9, when he says he will rise in France 'with so full glory/That I will dazzle all the eyes of France'. This contrasts with the king when a prince in *1 Henry IV* obscuring himself in 'base contagious clouds' (see p.66). The play also makes much use of images of soaring movement, of flights of birds, and parts of birds, suggesting Henry's swift rise to glory and the way it was achieved: 'Thus with imagined wing our swift scene flies / In motion of no less celerity / Than that of thought' (Chorus III, 1–3). The effect upon us is usually subconscious; we do not automatically register each image, clocking them up on some sort of emotional score-board. Their effect is almost insidious, causing us to respond in particular ways so that we respond as the author 'saw' his characters and their dilemmas.

A notable characteristic of the language in *Henry V* is its rhetorical variety. The Prologue begins the play in a manner that suggests this is no ramshackle chronicle of the earlier dramatic tradition but an epic; the language is appropriately hyperbolic (see Commentary). Chorus's use of hyperbole is even more telling in Chorus III. Scarcely any image is without an epithet. Not only is this luxuriance of qualification suggestive, but in the opening sentence, Shakespeare subtly prompts our imagination. Much of the description is designed to embroider fancy rather than offer simple information. Thus, 'brave' fleet, 'silken' streamers, 'shrill' whistle, the 'invisible and creeping' wind, 'huge' bottoms, 'furrowed' sea and 'lofty' surge, and so on to the 'nimble' gunner and his 'devilish' cannon. The richness of this description encourages the audience to 'see' via the images what cannot be shown on stage.

Such 'exaggerated' language can be contrasted with Pistol's bombast. *His* exaggeration undermines the character rather than reinforcing what is being conveyed. Then, between the Chorus's legitimate hyperbole and Pistol's absurd exaggeration, might be placed Henry's call to his men before Harfleur. Shakespeare gives the king lines which tread a narrow path between acceptable rhetoric and the sort of dramatic exaggeration which Shakespeare was to ridicule a year or two later when Hamlet recalls the 'rugged Pyrrhus' speech (see Commentary to III.i). Later in the seige, Henry demands the surrender of Harfleur in particularly violent language (III.iii). He outlines forcefully an attitude common to sixteenth-century warfare but this is to be understood almost as if it were wholly detached from character (see 3.4 and III.iii).

The contrast between prose and verse, used to dramatise both character and circumstance, is well shown in III.vi. Montjoy brings to Henry a final message from the King of France. Montjoy's contemptuous language is in prose and Henry's reply in verse. Montjoy can speak from a position of strength and Henry makes no bones about the enfeebled state of his army – yet it is Henry who wins this verbal contest, foreshadowing his winning the batle. Whereas Montjoy offers crude insult, Henry's rejoinder is beautifully and poetically turned. The English numbers are greatly reduced and those left 'Almost no better than so many French' (153) . . . but he brags, he says, and it must be the French air that has blown that vice into him! As if to counter Montjoy's gibe that Henry's exchequer is so poor (135), Henry generously sends the herald away with a purse for his pains.

In *Henry V*, language and character are intimately related and one cannot be considered apart from the other. Attention is drawn in the Commentary to subtleties of this relationship.

6.2 KING HENRY: CHARACTERISATION AND LANGUAGE

'Here is a play of action', says Granville-Barker, 'and here is the perfect man of action', but, he complains, there is 'very little that is dramatically interesting for him to do'. It is a rather strange judgement. That Henry is a man of action, resolute in the face of adversity, is true, but he is, surely, a very thoughtful character. The poet Swinburne described Henry as the noblest of a daring trio of 'calculating statesmen-warriors', one of whom was Cesare Borgia (C. 47). At the end of the first scene in which we see Henry as a young prince (*1 Henry IV*, I.ii. 192–215), Henry appears to behave in the most blatantly calculating manner, so much so that unsympathetic critics call him a hypocrite. Swinburne had in mind the Henry of the early part of *Henry V*. He argues that 'the future conqueror of Agincourt has practically made up his mind before he seeks . . . good reasons or . . . plausible excuse' to invade France.

There *was* a measure of cold calculation about members of the House of Lancaster and Henry V was not without that characteristic, but Shakespeare, whilst recognising that, is at pains to show him as no mere politician, no mere manipulator of men. This long meditation comes at the end of a night in which Henry has been shown inspecting his army at all levels. He has discussed their dangerous plight with his nobles; been challenged by Pistol; overheard Gower and Fluellen; and joined in discussion with three private soldiers troubled not only by their parlous state but by the rightness of the king's cause. Henry evaded directly answering Williams's doubts at the time (see Commentary on IV.i.135), and that marks the politician in him, the 'calculation' of which Swinburne speaks. That Williams's point was not lost on him, however, is apparent from the first lines of the king's soliloquy:

> Upon the King! Let us our lives, our souls,
> Our debts, our careful wives,
> Our children, and our sins, lay on the King!
> We must bear all. O hard condition!
> 240   Twin-born with greatness, subject to the breath
> Of every fool, whose sense no more can feel
> But his own wringing! What infinite heart's-ease
> Must kings neglect that private men enjoy!
> And what have kings that privates have not too,
> 245   Save ceremony, save general ceremony?
> And what art thou, thou idol ceremony?
> What kind of god art thou, that suffer'st more
> Of mortal griefs than do thy worshippers?
> What are thy rents? What are thy comings-in?
> 250   O ceremony, show me but thy worth!
> What is thy soul of adoration?
> Art thou aught else but place, degree, and form,
> Creating awe and fear in other men?
> Wherein thou art less happy, being feared,
> 255   Than they in fearing.

What drink'st thou oft, instead of homage sweet,
But poisoned flattery? O be sick, great greatness,
And bid thy ceremony give thee cure!
Think'st thou the fiery fever will go out
260 With titles blown from adulation?
Will it give place to flexure and low bending?
Canst thou, when thou command'st the beggar's
    knee,
Command the health of it? No, thou proud dream,
That play'st so subtly with a king's repose.
265 I am a king that find thee; and I know
'Tis not the balm, the sceptre, and the ball,
The sword, the mace, the crown imperial,
The intertissued robe of gold and pearl,
The farcèd title running 'fore the king,
270 The throne he sits on, nor the tide of pomp
That beats upon the high shore of this world—
No, not all these, thrice-gorgeous ceremony,
Not all these, laid in bed majestical,
Can sleep so soundly as the wretched slave,
275 Who with a body filled and vacant mind,
Gets him to rest, crammed with distressful bread;
Never sees horrid night, the child of hell;
But, like a lackey, from the rise to set,
Sweats in the eye of Phoebus, and all night
280 Sleeps in Elysium; next day after dawn,
Doth rise and help Hyperion to his horse,
And follows so the ever-running year
With profitable labour to his grave;
And but for ceremony, such a wretch,
285 Winding up days with toil and nights with sleep,
Had the forehand and vantage of a king.
The slave, a member of the country's peace,
Enjoys it; but in gross brain little wots
What watch the king keeps to maintain the peace,
290 Whose hours the peasant best advantages. (236–290)

Williams's question is now to be taken up. Shakespeare dramatises a king deeply anxious about his responsibilities to others and about the nature of the authority he wields. He contrasts the twin aspects of a monarch: the greatness of his position, but yet himself a subject to the whim of every fool. It is noticeable that prior to suggesting that a king may be equated with 'private man plus ceremony', Shakespeare touches on the paradox that he is born both monarch and subject – so twin-born. Further, the monarch, despite his power, can never enjoy the freedom of spirit (heart's ease) which plain subjects may. Shakespeare uses the word 'neglect' in a skilful way. We think of neglecting a duty; Henry here speaks of neglecting 'infinite heart's ease'; a true king can never neglect duty.

Henry now comes to the main burden of his meditation. What is special about a king is ceremony: it is only ceremony that makes a king different from ordinary individuals, he argues. Ceremony is then described and defined. The most telling description for an audience living within a Christian framework, is that of ceremony as a false god. Ceremony is but an idol (and Shakespeare probably has a pun in mind – thou idle ceremony), something fit only for pagans. This is a remarkable assertion given the medieval and Tudor concept (still practised at coronations in Britain) of the anointing of kings, a tradition that goes back to King David in the Old Testament. It is, suggests Henry, a hollow god that suffers more than his worshippers.

Henry then runs through a catalogue of ceremony's claims to be valuable. What rents is it paid? What receipts (comings-in) are credited to it? What *soul* to be worshipped has this idol (again suggesting a pagan relic)? Is ceremony any more than an empty form that creates fear in others, a fear that brings no happiness to the person feared? A king is more likely to be offered the poison of flattery than genuine homage and Henry asks whether ceremony can cure a king's sickness. This, and the lines that follow (257–63), are closely akin a Falstaff on the emptiness of honour, as he sees it, in *1 Henry IV*:

Can honour set to a leg? No. Or an arm? No. Or take away the grief of a wound? No. Honour hath no skill in surgery then? No. What is honour? A word. What is in that word honour? Air. A trim reckoning! (131–5)

So too, ceremony cannot cure a sickness, a fever, or make a king's knee as healthy as one bent in respect to him by someone begging a favour. Ceremony is no more than a proud dream (compare honour = air), no fitter than to disturb the dreamer's sleep. All those symbols that represent royalty, the gorgeous apparel, the pomp accorded those in the highest reaches of society, cannot enable the possessor to sleep as soundly, however fine the bed, as the most wretched, but vacant-minded subject, who has earned by his daily labour the wherewithal to fill his stomach. Such a subject is too tired from hard work (running like a lackey alongside the chariot of Phoebus, the sun-god) ever to witness the horrors of the night, which Henry in his wretchedness equates with hell, a traditional association as in *The Rape of Lucrece*:

> Frantic with grief thus breathes she forth her spite
> Against the unseen secrecy of night
> 'O comfort-killing night, image of hell . . .
> Black stage for tragedies and murders fell . . .' (762–4,766)

A subject sleeps as in heaven (Elysium), unlike the king, wakeful in the hell of night, and can thus arise refreshed, to labour again, symbolically helping the sun-god to harness the horses of his chariot for another day's journey across the sky. Thus can he profitably work through the years of his life. (The sun-god went by several names. Helios was, properly, the God of the Sun. He was the son of Hyperion but was frequently given his father's name. Phoebus, the Shining One, was an epithet given Apollo, representing the idea of light in his function as God of the Year and its Months.)

The ordinary labourer, argues Henry, is better-placed in these respects than is the king. What is more, he enjoys his peaceful life only because the king keeps nightly watch to maintain that peace, something which the peasant's coarse and stupid brain cannot conceive.

Paraphrased in detail, Henry's comparison of his state with that of a peasant's life might seem self-pitying. That is not in accord with the tone of the soliloquy. Henry is not arguing that the harshness of the peasant's life is preferable to the luxury in which he lives, but contrasting the difference in responsibility and the effect that has on peace of mind. What Henry attempts is to tease out what characterises a monarch, how the differences in a king's state and a subject's are derived, and how that affects them. Behind the speech is an element of conventional wisdom. Rulers who took their duties seriously were expected to lie awake at night worrying (see p.16). Shakespeare also draws a sharp distinction between the nature of a king and that of a private individual. The description of what makes a king different – ceremony – seems to suggest that far from being semi-divine, ceremony is but an idol, a hollow god, a fantasy. In dramatising this issue, Shakespeare is incorporating into the early fifteenth century late sixteenth-century theories. He does this with consummate tact, for the issues were extremely sensitive. So far as Henry's character is concerned, that he should be so troubled in this way makes it plain that he is by no means merely a calculating manipulator, nor solely a man of action. Rather can we see the great advance the king has made since, as a young prince, he first unburdened himself of his intentions in *1 Henry IV*. He then proposed 'to imitate the sun' obscured by 'base contagious clouds' so that when he was revealed in his full glory he could trick expectancy (I.ii.196–209).

Working out the implications of what is said presents only one aspect of this speech. Equally important is the way that Shakespeare expressed Henry's argument. Shakespeare is not writing a political tract (which is what explication might make the speech appear to be), but dramatic poetry. The key device Shakespeare employs is repetition, but he uses it in such a way that he is never guilty of *mere* repetition. He creates verbal and rhythmic patterns that drive home the argument, sustain interest, and ensure understanding.

Shakespeare begins with a simple statement of the complex issues raised by the private soldiers, all concentrated into a three-word phrase: 'Upon the king'. Then begins the technique of repetition. There are half-a-dozen instances of what is being laid upon the king and a near-repetition of the very first phrase, each instance introduced by 'our'. This contrast between the king and his responsibilities on the one hand, and his subjects on the other, is thus convincingly epitomised as a 'hard condition' and the abruptness of this description enforces our awareness of how Henry feels his position. A second sequence of repetitions begins with 'What infinite heart's ease'. There are no fewer than eight questions. Directly and indirectly these tease out the nature of ceremony which is itself then dissected in a sequence of ten negatives. The increasing number of repetitions, from six to eight to ten, take upwards of three-quarters of the speech, building tension and momentum. They are then summarised in further repeated negatives – 'No, not all these . . . Not all these'. – The last quarter of the speech is quite different in structure. It is devoted to the subject, in contrast to the first three-quarters, which was focused on the king. It is one long complex sentence, without repetition, and its style provides as much contrast with what has gone before as there is between their subjects: king and 'slave'. Thus, all the attributes of kingship are questioned and viewed negatively whereas there is a continuous and positive description of the peasant. The last four lines of the speech are a sort of coda on peace (contrasting with the occasion that has provoked the king's meditation, the forthcoming battle), and the relationship of king and

peasant thereto. In these ways, the styles of rhetoric, sentence
lengths, and the structure of the speech, combine to express the
contrast between king and subject, and between the king's 'two
bodies' (see 5.5), which are dramatised in this soliloquy.

7 THE ROLE OF COMEDY IN *HENRY V*

7.1 COMEDY AND LAUGHTER

We tend, hardly surprisingly, to equate comedy with laughter. One of the most famous studies of comedy, that by Henri Bergson, has in the original French the title, 'Le Rire, essai sur la signification due comique' (1900). The contemporary Theatre of Comedy concentrates on producing farces and it would not have achieved its great success, sometimes with as many as three productions running simultaneously in London, if it did not milk every moment for laughs. Despite that, comedy is not a simple matter of laughter. At the other extreme, one of Shakespeare's contemporaries, Ben Jonson, wrote:

the moving of laughter is a fault in comedy, a kind of turpitude that depraves some part of a man's nature without a disease.

The great comedies of Shakespeare, Congreve, Sheridan, and Wilde do raise much laughter (as does Jonson in his *Volpone* and *The Alchemist*), but none of them are simply concerned with raising laughs; Shakespeare's and Congreve's comedies have particularly serious dimensions. Even Shakespeare's most farcical comedy, *The Comedy of Errors*, runs quite deep below the surface.

Comedy has more to do with an attitude to life than with laughter, of life to be grasped, and how the trials and tribulations dramatised can be resolved within the framework of their society. That society will go on in much the same way, perhaps with one or two characters a little modified, its continuation suggested by the weddings, feasting, and dancing with one or more of which so many classical comedies conclude. That comedic ending is an earnest of the future.

Pre-Shakespearian chronicle plays are filled out with low comedy innocent of serious purpose. Horseplay, jokes, and comic confusions are interspersed between pageant-like scenes without too much regard for homogeneity of tone or purpose. Marlowe's *Dr Faustus* (a pseudo-biography rather than a chronicle) alternates serious and farce episodes and though they are given a loose connection (the folly of Dr Faustus contrasted with the relative commonsense of the clowns), as a dramatic structure the play is little advanced on a medieval mystery play which has one scene 'stuffed' inside another (*Noah and Lamech*). The original meaning of farce is stuffed (compare 'dindon farcie' – stuffed turkey), and it is clear that Shakespeare understood this meaning of farce from IV.i.269: 'the farced title running 'fore the king' (the lengthy style of address given a king into which one pompous title after another is stuffed). That this 'stuffing' of serious matter with irrelevant comedy was becoming out of fashion by 1590 is plain from the edition of Marlowe's *Tamberlaine* published in that year: the printer explained that he had purposely left out all the comic scenes because they 'would prove a great disgrace to so honourable and stately a history'. It was to be Shakespeare who showed how comedy should be used 'seriously' and, in *Henry V*, in a particularly effective and important manner.

7.2   THE SERIOUS USE OF COMEDY

One of Shakespeare's most creative insights was to grasp how comedy might be used in 'serious' drama. There are those who have deplored his fondness for certain comic elements. Thus Samuel Johnson on Shakespeare's propensity for punning:

> A quibble is to Shakespeare what luminous vapours are to the traveller; he follows it at all adventures; it is sure to lead him out of his way and sure to engulf him in the mire. It has some malignant power over his mind, and its fascinations are irresistible . . . . A quibble was to him the fatal Cleopatra for which he lost the world and was content to lose it.

Many academic critics studiously avoid consideration of Shakespeare's use of bad puns, but even this device is part and parcel of Shakespeare's grasp of the sophisticated role comedy can play in non-comedic drama. No one before or since has managed to do this so well. Because sometimes we come to such plays with a bland, undistinguishing, approach so far as their comedy is concerned, Shakespeare's subtle tonal variations can be missed. It is a commonplace that the comic tones of the first and second parts of *Henry IV* are different. The Falstaff of *2 Henry IV* is losing ground and his wit is nothing like as sharp as in *1 Henry IV*. This is not because Shakespeare's wit has become blunted: it is consonant with the nature of the third play of the tetralogy.

7.3 THE DEATH OF FALSTAFF

Even if William Kempe, chief clown of the Chamberlain's Men up until about the time of *Henry V*, was available to play Falstaff in this play (as Shakespeare had promised at the end of *2 Henry IV*), there were good artistic reasons for excluding the fat knight. His presence would have raised false expectations in audiences, expectations at odds with the comedy appropriate to *Henry V*. It is not that there are no grounds for laughter in *Henry V*. For example, the first eighty lines of II.i are comic enough as is most of V.i. In both these scenes there is a good combination of comic dialogue and comic business. Thus, as the two cowards, Nym and Pistol, draw their swords as if to duel, the Hostess's horror is expressed in comic confusion: 'we shall see wilful adultery and murder committed' (37). However, neither of these scenes concludes in so light a tone. With the entry of the Boy in II.i, the scene darkens. Falstaff is very sick: the king has killed his heart (82, 88). There are attempts at humour between these two lines – Bardolph's red nose shall serve to warm Falstaff's bed and the Hostess forecasts a gallows fate for the Boy ('he'll yield the crow a pudding', 87). It is too early in the play to take these as anything but comic, but the gallows will prove to be Bardolph's end, not the Boy's, and the Boy will almost certainly be one of those murdered at Agincourt.

The more-or-less comic quarrel continues after the Hostess and the Boy leave the stage to attend to Falstaff, but at her return it is plain that Falstaff's death approaches. It is difficult to be sure what Pistol means by Falstaff's heart being 'fracted and corroborate' (124) – perhaps Pistol himself is not intended to know – but Falstaff's heart is either broken and corrupted, or he has humbled his heart sufficiently to accept the grace of salvation. The latter would be a more generous conclusion for it would mean Falstaff would not be going the way the Vice invariably did: to Hell.

This first comic scene establishes a pattern that will be repeated several times. The comedy often has a sour note and, time and again, it is juxtaposed with death. As comedy is a genre which dramatises 'life to be grasped', such a juxtaposition is bitterly ironic. Jonson's description of laughter as a fault in comedy, though not wholly applicable, seems not *quite* so strange in this context.

The next comic scene is II.iii. This starts with an account of Falstaff's death and continues with the Hostess's sympathetic description of his last moments. It is a curious mixture of pathos and comic confusion. The scene concludes with a suggestion of the comic roguery of Gadshill in *1 Henry IV* (I.ii and II.ii) but soured by unhealthy parasitism:

> Yoke-fellows in arms,
> Let us to France; like horse-leeches, my boys,
> To suck, to suck, the very blood to suck! (55–7)

7.4 BEFORE HARFLEUR

The next appearance of the three comics, in III.iii, has been described in some detail in the Commentary. Here the comedy serves to undercut – or at least, provide a different perspective to – the epic pretensions of this gallant enterprise. It is important that Henry should not be wholly undermined. Shakespeare crafts a delicate balance between the heroic, 'Once more, unto the breach, dear friends' and Bardolph's parody. In the long run it is Henry's call to his compatriots that sticks in the mind whilst Bardolph and his jeer are lost to memory, but momentarily we are given pause to think what it is that is being ventured rather than being carried along unthinkingly by the king's enthusiasm.

7.5 THE COMEDY OF ACCENT

III.ii also introduces us to all four 'comic' captains. It is easy to see why this little cameo was given prominence in Olivier's wartime film. It *does* provide comedy, although critics have objected that Shakespeare's attitude to these representatives of the four nations, especially his Welsh and Irish captains, is condescending, but in 1942–44 it could easily be made to represent the four nations of Britain joined in a worthy enterprise. (It was at this time, incidentally, long before the institution itself was set up, that President Roosevelt took to referring to the Allies as 'The United Nations' in order to overcome American constitutional objections to forming alliances.) But why are the captains treated as figures of comedy?

Whereas much of the comedy in *Henry V* is associated with unpleasant characteristics, *this* comedy is intended optimistically. As mentioned above (1.2) and below (8.2), the ideal of a union of the four nations was advocated by the Earl of Essex. Dramatising that in a brief scene presented Shakespeare with problems. He was writing for an English (not British) audience and though Wales had been joined with England under the Tudors, Scotland was a foreign country and England was waging war in Ireland at the time the play was written and first performed. The campaign was being led by Essex; he had set forth on 27 March 1599 and was to return in less than triumph on 28 September 1599. Between these dates Shakespeare evidently wrote the reference to Essex in the Chorus to Act V, 30–4.

The English have found people of different countries, and even those from different counties of England, either funny or contemptible. There is ample evidence for this going back to at least the poems of Laurence Minot in the early fourteenth century and although attempts to modify this by legislation are now being tried, it continues to this day. In a review of the RSC 1975 production, Harold Hobson wrote in the *Sunday Times* that this play suffers a great handicap for contemporary audiences in that it glories in being English. He continued:

> Now to glory in being Welsh, Scottish, or Irish is permissible, and even laudable. But to be proud of being English is generally regarded as bordering on indecency: it makes the delicate blush. (B.250–1)

Shakespeare wished to show the four countries united in action. He was doubtless aware of the military etiquette of the time that endeavoured to ensure that an army composed of different nationals did not suffer from internal squabbling. That must make for strain, however (just as in a United Nations Peacekeeping Force). Finally, at least two of the countries involved were regarded by the English with deep suspicion (an attitude reciprocated in turn). The comedy which might strike a false note for us enabled Shakespeare to show his four representative captains united in common cause. In this Shakespeare is remarkably prescient, just as he is in dramatising Macmorris's anguished cries, 'What ish my nation? Who talks of my nation?'

7.6 DEATHS OF THE COMICS

The most curious aspect of the team of low comics Shakespeare brings together for *Henry V* is their fate. Consider first the numbers of English reported killed at Agincourt (presumably omitting the murdered baggage boys): 29. We know that there were probably 400–500 killed but 29 was the figure in Shakespeare's sources and is the total he gives (IV.viii. 105–8). Now contrast the fates of the quartet which includes the three comics. Nym and Bardolph are hanged (IV.iv. 75) and the Boy is presumably numbered amongst the dead baggage boys. The RSC production in 1975 did, as have many productions, include the Boy among those murdered, having his body carried on stage for Henry to recognise (especially as he had played Francis in *1* and *2 Henry IV*). Add to these the reported deaths of Falstaff and Nell (or Doll – see Commentary) and it must be agreed that wholly against precedent the comics get very short shrift in this play. It is rare for a clown to be killed in Elizabethan and Jacobean drama. It must, therefore, be asked why Shakespeare should so treat his clowns in *Henry V*. One implication is that all but one of Hal's boon companions of his profligate youth have departed the scene (and Pistol appeared late, half-way through *2 Henry IV*). It also indicates that the gaiety of Falstaff's 'court' in *1 Henry IV* has no place in the world of Agincourt and Troyes. It means, too, that jolly humour has no place in the grim scene of war. Shakespeare goes to some trouble to change the image of war from adventure and even game – the 'game's afoot' of III.i. 32. This can be made even plainer in the way a newly introduced, if unwitting, comic – le Fer – is presented, especially in some productions.

7.7 COMEDY AND THE KILLING OF PRISONERS

The only scene demanding fighting specified by Shakespeare is that which involves Monsieur le Fer and Pistol, although directions for 'Alarums' at four later points give an opportunity for displays of fighting that most directors like to develop. There is nothing, however, like the fight between Henry V (when Prince Hal) and Hotspur, or Henry IV and Douglas in *1 Henry IV*, V.iv. This is the only contest that has dialogue and thus Shakespeare throws a fair amount of weight on to this scene. Though a battle scene, it is comic. As Terry Hands, Director of the RSC 1975 production explained:

> This is an inescapably funny scene. We rehearsed it serious, savage, slow. It just got funnier . . . The clattering of puns drowns that of [the] armour [of the] symbolic M. le Fer (Mr. Iron) (B.196)

Of course, Shakespeare doesn't think a battle is funny. Rather he is behaving like the old Vice of the Morality Drama – having us enjoy what is really far removed from the enjoyable. We witness this part of the battle as sheer entertainment, and then the rug is pulled from under our feet when we realise the true implications of war: killing boys and cutting prisoners' throats.

Although there is no authority for it in the text, the RSC in 1975 made up a scene by combining a couple of lines from the beginning of V.vii ('Kill the poys and the luggage? 'Tis expressly against the law of arms' and Gower's "Tis certain there's not a boy left alive'); followed by lines 57–61 of that scene (Henry's 'I was not angry since I came to France . . . they do offend our sight'); then switching back to the last three lines spoken by Henry in IV.vi, but giving the first of these to Exeter ('The French have reinforced their scattered men!'), and finally Henry's order that the prisoners' throats be cut. In Holinshed's account of the battle, the orders to kill the prisoners are confused and Shakespeare makes them no clearer (see Commentary). This rearrangement of the lines (which is backed by a rather specious line of argument in the footnotes to the RSC's version, B.201), gives a double justification for the king's order that is certainly not in the play Shakespeare wrote. What the RSC then did might well be said to be thoroughly in the spirit of the play. At Agincourt, a picked body of 200 archers killed the prisoners. Shakespeare gives no directions that we are to witness this horrible event. In 1975, the RSC, on the ground that the one prisoner we did know about was M. le Fer, had Pistol cut his throat immediately upon Henry's 'Give the word throughout' (IV.vi. 38). The play then continued from the line following on from that already spoken by Fluellen ("Tis an arrant piece of knavery').

Whether or not directors are entitled so to rearrange Shakespeare's plays, it can be argued that the way M. le Fer is killed in this production does carry out Shakespeare's intentions in a general sense. This comic character wins the instant affection of the audience, partly because of his comic accent (which can help endear a character as well as cause him to be ridiculed), partly because we know he has been captured by a thorough scoundrel (and compare the taking prisoner of Sir John Colevile of the Dale by Falstaff at Gaultree Forest in *2 Henry IV*, IV.iii), and partly because of the Boy's soliloquy, the second given to this minor character. The RSC neatly juxtaposed the killing of the Boy by the looters (immediately after his soliloquy), and the killing of le Fer, thirty lines later. We are thus witness to the untimely deaths of two attractive characters. There can be little doubt that the comedy of le Fer's capture was designed to endear him to us and his death is thus the more shocking.

7.8 PISTOL'S COMEUPPANCE

Because this account tends to draw out the darker uses of comedy, it might be thought that this is how all the comedy is to be interpreted, as if, in Jonson's words, laughter were a fault. However, for the comedy to have its 'dark' effect, it must also prompt laughter. We should laugh at the Hostess and Pistol in II.i and iii; we are certainly meant to find accents funny, even though we may think we are above that sort of thing nowadays, whether those of the captains, Katharine and Alice, or M. le Fer; Pistol and the latter can hardly be other than funny; and we get a certain sardonic pleasure from the way in which Fluellen teaches the wretched Pistol a lesson in V.i. That, plainly, is a comic scene although again Shakespeare goes out of his way to introduce death, disease, and skulduggery into Pistol's *envoi* (which can usefully be compared to Pandarus's last speech in *Troilus and Cressida*). This scene might also go some way towards answering the charge sometimes made of Shakespeare's alleged condescension towards those whose accents are not that of Standard English. Apart from the favour generally shown Wales and the Welsh in this play – Harry's proud claim to be Welsh (he was born at Monmouth), the sturdily independent Williams, and Fluellen's valour – this scene not only shows the triumph of the accent-full Fluellen, but Gower's condemnation of the mocking of an ancient tradition. Shakespeare even makes the point that people are not to be judged by their accent:

> *Gower*: You thought, because he could not speak English in the native garb, he could not therefore handle an English cudgel. You find it otherwise, and henceforth let a Welsh correction teach you a good English condition. (V.i. 78–82)

7.9 THE FRANKNESS OF BURGUNDY'S MIRTH

Enough has already been said about the comedy of Kate's language lesson in the Commentary to III.iv not to require more to be said here than that its comedy invariably charms audiences and Shakespeare performs another clever balancing act as he so delicately presents indelicacy. A little more attention needs to be given to Burgundy's 'mirth' in the last scene of the play to which that language lesson is related.

The significance of the syllable 'con' is made clear in the English language lesson, for it is this, and the English word 'foot', that cause Katharine's outburst that words she takes to be four-letter obscenities are bad, corruptible, gross and shameful – though she manages to voice them twice more. Now what is it in what Henry has just said that Burgundy finds need to answer and to excuse himself for the frankness [openness/Frenchness] of his mirth – and why mirth? Henry has just complained that he cannot 'so conjure up the spirit of love in her [Kate], that he [Love] will appear in his true likeness' (307–8). The word 'conjure' must be deliberately chosen because of that syllable 'con' (instead of, say, 'rouse') because 'conjure' is immediately repeated twice by Burgundy and twice more in that same speech he has words including that syllable: 'condition' and 'consign'. Shortly after we have 'consent(ed)' thrice and also Henry's 'I am content' (344). The 'frankness' of Burgundy's mirth now begins to look very like bawdy, hence his begging pardon. [It is ironic, incidentaly, that the New Arden editor should substitute 'conjure' for the usual eighteenth-century emendation, 'summon' in Henry's 'Once more, unto the breach' speech at III.i. 7.] This is not done to elicit cheap laughter from the unthinking but is, to adapt the title of Adrian Colman's book on the subject, a dramatic use of bawdy in Shakespeare (see Further Reading). Coupled with the reference to flies at Bartholomew-tide, to handling (and see 5.1, p.53 above), the verbal onslaught of Henry's wooing and the equation by Henry of Kate with French cities to be taken, this 'mirth' has anything but a laugh-raising function. Here, Jonson's 'laughter is a fault in comedy' would apply.

The end of romantic comedy is marriage and reconciliation and we seem to have just such a comedic end to this play, but it is far from unalloyed happiness. The tone of this part of V.ii anticipates that of the dark comedies which were immediately to follow *Henry V*. (Note how at the end of *Measure for Measure* there is no specific indication that Isabella and the Duke will marry; some directors have them exit hand in hand; others (more correctly?), have them leave the stage in different directions.)

It is a pity that we are so wedded to the idea of the glorious, epic hero (which Shakespeare does also dramatise) that directors feel unable to persuade audiences to come to terms with Shakespeare's sour, almost cynical, ending which presages the loss of France and England's shedding of so much blood during the reign of Henry's son, with which thoughts the Chorus bids us adieu. It is a measure of Shakespeare's genius that he can offer us both views simultaneously and it is not beyond audiences to apprehend both together. W. B. Yeats, although he wrote so disparagingly of *Henry V*, did put his finger on one important characteristic of the play. Shakespeare, he said, 'spoke his tale, as he spoke all his tales, with tragic irony' (C.55). That we can find most distinctly at the end of V.ii.

Following the 1964 RSC production of *Henry V*, the dramatist John Arden suggested that the 'surface view' of the play – he described it as 'Agincourt was a lovely war' – had many corrections within the structure of the play, so much so that we must wonder if Shakespeare hadn't written 'a secret play within the official one' (something he said he himself did). The use of comedy in *Henry V*, and especially the conclusion to the final scene, are just such 'corrections within the structure'.

8 OLIVIER'S FILM OF

HENRY V

8.1 STAGE AND FILM

Stage performances are ephemeral. Photographs can help a little to recapture what settings and costumes looked like; a recording of a performance before a regular audience can tell the critic much, but as the quality of such recordings is poor, they are infrequently made for sale to the general public. It is a remarkably different experience to listen to Richard Burton's commercial gramophone recording of his 1964 New York *Hamlet* and to watch a filmed record, made by a static camera, positioned in the stalls, of an actual performance. Neither gives the full experience of being *there* and each is very different from the other. We know from comparing what newspaper critics tell us that very often the last thing one can imagine is that they have all attended the same performance. Despite that, we tend to take as fact accounts by eighteenth- and nineteenth-century critics of the way great actors interpreted their roles. It is quite a shock to listen to a recording made in 1890 of Edwin Booth's Othello – a role he played opposite Sir Henry Irving's Iago, the two actors exchanging roles for successive performances – after reading accounts of how he acted and in particular his proneness to rant. Through the crackle of that century-old recording it is possible to make out a wonderfully modulated and calmly measured delivery! Theatre, in brief, is for experiencing in the flesh. It needs an audience to complete the event. For those who would appreciate drama to the full, no other medium, not even the 'theatre in the mind', is an adequate substitute.

In the above, I have carefully skirted round film. What of Shakespeare adapted for the cinema? (I am not including in this a filmed record of a theatre production by a static camera.) What, especially, of one of the most famous Shakespeare adaptations for the cinema: Olivier's *Henry V* (1944)?

First, film is *different* from theatre. It is not worse; it is not better; it is different. The experience of witnessing a film can be repeated and though the audience's apprehensions may change – contrast the response of a twenty-year-old and a sixty-year-old to a film made forty years ago – the film remains the same. Theatrical performances change with each re-presentation as actors 'feel out' their audiences. Film directors know that, once completed, their films will not change and so they make their films with that permanency, that 'fixed image', in mind. [Of course, sometimes changes are made to films to suit everything from the censor's frown to the advertising break, but these are not changes made at the director's instigation.] A very simple example of the difference in approach might be useful. In a comedy, an actor in the theatre will carefully time his lines, (a) to get the best response, and (b) to ensure that the next line is not drowned by laughter for otherwise the point may be lost. In film, the timing once settled cannot be varied so a director must control his medium to allow for a response, yet be aware there may be little or none, and still keep the pace moving. Curiously, a film audience will often discipline itself to accord with the narrative pace in a way that theatre audiences rarely do.

It is, therefore, very important to distinguish theatre-going and film-going experiences and not to equate the two. Seeing a film or television production of *Henry V* is not the same as *participating in a production* as a member of a theatre audience. As long as that is appreciated, a film version can be very helpful to the study of a play-text. It is to be hoped that everyone studying *Henry V* will see Olivier's film. If the provisos just given are borne in mind, and the viewer is aware of the circumstances attendant upon the making of that film, there is much to be learned and enjoyed. As the film can be bought in video form, or hired for a pound or two, there is no reason why it should not be seen by everyone with access to a video recorder (though seeing a film on video is not *quite* the same as seeing a film in a cinema).

8.2 WARTIME PROPAGANDA AND *HENRY V*

It is vital to appreciate that Olivier's film was conceived early in 1942 and was made in 1943 and 1944. It was proposed when Britain's fortunes were at a very low ebb. Rommel had swept all before him in North Africa; Singapore had fallen to the Japanese and they were making for India; the Russians were falling back on Stalingrad. It was a very, very dismal time indeed. When Dallas Bower suggested to Olivier early in 1942 that *Henry V* be filmed, Olivier responded enthusiastically and, as Harry Geduld, the author of a Filmguide to this production, puts it, that response was, in part, 'due to Olivier's immediate recognition that a film of *Henry V* could be given topical (propagandist) relevance'. From the start there was a conscious propaganda aspect to this film. No wonder that the union of the four nations through Fluellen, Gower, Jamy, and Macmorris is so indelibly conveyed – a union advocated 350 years earlier by the ill-fated Earl of Essex (see 1.2). This propagandist dimension was reinforced by the use of colour. In Britain at that time, because of wartime shortages, colour film was very rarely made available. (Another exception at this time was a Government-sponsored, propaganda film on the Atlantic sea-lanes, *Western Approaches*.) Thus, the first audiences saw this as a very special film, especially when they read the film's dedication to the commandos and airborne troops of Great Britain. The film had its première on 22 November 1944, two months after the First British Airborne Division was dropped at Arnhem.

8.3 THE GLOBE RECONSTRUCTED

At a time when the average film ran for about ninety minutes, Olivier had to cut the length of *Henry V* pretty savagely, especially as he was adding re-enacted battle scenes. Even so the film runs for 2½ hours. Further, if 'Shakespeare audiences' at the Memorial Theatre in Stratford found the opening slow, Olivier felt he had to take precautions to prevent a mass audience being bored. He did three things, therefore. He cut the text; he introduced comic by-play (e.g. the Bishop of Ely's 'business', dropping the Archbishop's papers and then hunting on the floor for the next part of the speech); and, what proved a touch of genius, he started the play off in a reconstructed Globe Theatre, showing also an Elizabethan audience and the hectic preparations backstage.

This gives the film a special, if rather dangerous, value for it does convey some impression of what conditions were like when Shakespeare's plays were first performed. It serves the immediate task of providing an alternative source of interest to those who find what the Archbishop has to say unexciting and it also gives those accustomed only to a nineteenth-century style theatre a fresh perspective on staging. It is easy for scholars to hum and ha and say (as I would), 'Oh, *that* isn't correct', and, 'Oh, we don't *really* know about that', but we do get the feel of an early production and, astonishingly, Olivier's temerity sparked off renewed interest in scholars on both sides of the Atlantic in Elizabethan theatres. So, *this* Globe is a guess, not established fact – but it is an inspired guess.

8.4 THE IDEALISATION OF HENRY V

Olivier also cuts the last scene severely and so, coupled with the propagandist element, we get a too good, too noble, almost saintly Henry. Note, for example, the 'halo effect' of the golden crown round the king's helmet! This is not a *wrong* interpretation so far as it goes, but it is limited and partial. Despite that, such is the conviction with which Olivier carries it through that, in its own terms, it works brilliantly. But it is not the whole play.

8.5 NON-REALISTIC SETTINGS

One final point about the film is worth noting. Films are nearly always imitations of actuality. One of the aspects of this film that is different from any play is that the Battle of Agincourt is re-enacted with seemingly hundreds of soldiers and cavalry. (Probably, although 'official' figures vary, some 180 cavalry were used and 500 infantry, provided by the Eirean Home Guard; the battle scenes could not be filmed in England because of interference from low-flying aircraft.) We also have what seems to be a 'real' Globe Theatre, and that, too, is a convention of film. Things look as they are supposed to be. However (and this is another touch of Olivier's genius), when it came to showing the French Court, Olivier eschewed actuality and used painted backgrounds based on medieval illuminations in *Les Très Riches Heures du Duc de Berri* (begun for the very Duke of Berri who appears in the play). These marvellously evoke the period in which the events took place. Because the originals were in German-Occupied France, reproductions from a calendar were pressed into service.

8.6 AN AMERICAN RESPONSE TO OLIVIER'S FILM

Many people have written about this film but the best short comment was made at the time by an American poet, James Agee, whom Harry Geduld quotes at the conclusion of his Filmguide:

I am not a Tory, a monarchist, a Catholic, a medievalist, an Englishman, or, despite all the good that it engenders, a lover of war: but the beauty and power of this traditional exercise was such that, watching it, I wished I was, thought I was, and was proud of it.

I was persuaded, and in part still am, that every time and place has since been in decline, save one, in which one Englishman used language better than anyone has before or since, or ever shall; and that nearly the best that our time can say for itself is that some of us are still capable of paying homage to the fact.

9 CRITICAL RECEPTION

As so often with Shakespeare's plays and those of his contemporaries, there are not as many references as we should like to performances in his lifetime. We can reasonably conjecture from the references to Essex's campaign in Ireland (see 7.5) that *Henry V* was first performed in the spring or early summer of 1599, probably at the Curtain Theatre, the Globe not being ready until late summer of 1599 (see Commentary to Prologue). The first definite record of a performance is of one given at Court on 7 January 1605 as part of the Christmas Revels. No more is heard of performances until the adaptation of the play by Aaron Hill in 1723, the comic characters being omitted and replaced by a sentimental subplot featuring Scroop and a new character, Harriet. Twelve years later Shakespeare's version was presented and it has been given regularly since. Most of the famous English actors have played Henry and it is one of a small group of plays adapted to include a coronation procession (in 1767), and there have sometimes been special coronation productions (as in 1937). Although it has often been an excuse for lavish productions, the opposite tendencies can also be found. Terry Hands, director of the 1975 RSC production, began the play with his actors gathering on stage some half-an-hour before the play was timed to start. They were dressed in rehearsal clothes and the stage was completely bare. Gradually, the play worked towards a conventionally-dressed production as the action proceeded, the first sign of change being the moment when Canterbury greeted the king (I.ii.7). As he did so, as Mr Hands notes, 'he opens his jacket to reveal a pectoral cross' (B. 106). This production was one of four plays (the others being the three 'Falstaff' plays, *1* and *2 Henry IV* and *The Merry Wives of Windsor*) chosen to celebrate the centenary of the Shakespeare Memorial Theatre at Stratford. The key to Hands's approach was to be lines 15–26 of the Prologue. The aim was to prompt audiences' collaboration to 'deck our kings'. Not all the critics were impressed favourably. *The Times* described the opening as a stylistic oddity, seeing the cast as so many football referees whilst the audience was supposed to eke out the stage designer's imperfections with their thoughts (B. 250). In an Afterword to the book on the production, Ronald Bryden explained that one reason for the limited use of settings was financial, but the real reason lay elsewhere:

> If audiences would accept the convention of actors in modern dress informing them that they were actors, not dead mediaeval worthies, about to tell the tale of Agincourt without illusion, it might be possible to play *Henry IV*, *Parts One* and *Two* as Shakespeare wrote them to be performed. (B. 247)

Leaving aside the irony of the words 'as Shakespeare wrote them to be performed' following the production of a play in which a pretty free hand had been applied to the text (see, for example, 7.7), this did show a contemporary audience that spectacular scenery, realistic trappings, dioramas, and the like were not essential to the play; indeed, they may distract an audience from some of the play's complexities of tone.

The play has, not surprisingly, been presented with particular, if one-sided, appeal in time of war – the Boer War, the First World War, and the 1939–45 War are twentieth-century examples. Reading descriptions of the stirringly patriotic representations of Henry V given by Lewis Waller in the first decades of this century, or listening to a recording by him made in 1911 of 'Once more, unto the breach', makes one realise how relatively restrained is Olivier's film for its time. The play (not just its opening) was given entirely in modern dress in 1960 (by Bernard Miles at the Mermaid Theatre, Blackfriars), and also at Blackfriars it was played under glaring white lights in 1936 under Robert Atkins's direction. There was an all-woman production by Marie Slade's company in 1916; it has been given by youth theatres and in the open air, in Regent's Park, London, for example.

Henry V is an easy play to present when patriotism runs high; it is less easy if a director lacks the simple certainty of a Lewis Waller, and if he lacks audiences such as those Waller addressed, who rose cheering to their feet every time he gave the St Crispin's Day speech (IV.iii. 40–67). That should not disguise the fact that productions truer to Shakespeare are probably more readily attainable in less jingoistic times.

Critics, too, have responded with unease to a simple faith in this very English epic. As early as 1817, William Hazlitt, who expressed strong dislike of the historical Henry V – 'he was careless, dissolute, and ambitious . . . he seemed to have no idea of the common decencies of life' – wrote:

> Henry V it is true, was a hero . . . Yet we feel little love or admiration for him. . . . How then do we like him? We like him in the play. There is he a very amiable monster, a very splendid pageant. As we like to gaze at a panther or a young lion in their cages in the Tower, and catch a pleasing horror from their glistening eyes, their velvet paws, and dreadless roar, so we take a very romantic, heroic, patriotic, and poetical delight in the boasts and feats of our younger Harry, as they appear on the stage and are confined to lines of ten syllables; where no blood follows the stroke that wounds our ears, where no harvest bends beneath horses' hoofs, no city flames, no little child is butchered, no dead men's bodies found piled on heaps and festering the next morning – in the orchestra! (C. 37)

Half a century later, Thomas Kenny argued that the subject of *Henry V* 'did not admit of perfect dramatic treatment' and the character of the king could not itself be dramatic because Henry was 'exhibited as a complete, harmonious, self-possessed character' (C.41). Alan Howard, who played the king in 1975, showed that the king could be exhibited as anything but self-possessed but rather a man racked by doubts. Who is right? Harley Granville-Barker, one of the greatest combined practitioners and theoreticians of Shakespeare, seems to follow Kenny:

> No one could say that Henry is ill-drawn or uninteresting. But, when it comes to the point, there seems to be very little that is dramatically interesting for him to do. Here is a play of action, and here is the perfect man of action. (C. 62)

But, *does* Henry have so little to do that is dramatically interesting? *Is* the play so taken up with action?

When all is said and done, the third group to receive Shakespeare's plays after the theatricals and critics have done has to be considered: the audience. Hazlitt is here surely right: 'Henry V is a very favourite monarch with the English nation, and he appears to have been also a favourite with Shakespeare' (C. 36). It may be that audiences tend to be middle-class and rather traditional, expecting and responding to the more patriotic aspects of the play, but the appeal of *Henry V* has been long-lasting and has proved itself in times of patriotic fervour (for example, in the first years of this century), and also in much less confident times, such as the 1930s and the past two decades. Probably Hazlitt is right: Shakespeare did delight in his hero and that delight comes through in his writing and it is that which carries the audience with him.

The doubts and qualifications of critics and directors are not, however, so easily to be dismissed. If *Henry V* were no more than a jingoistic exercise, then the carpings of Yeats and George Bernard Shaw and John Masefield and Mark Van Doren, and others, would be more than justified. But the play has much more to it, and Henry is more complex, than their responses allow. Without making Henry a prototype Hamlet, Shakespeare does show Henry as more intelligent, anxious, and sensitive than a grossly material hero could possibly be. Unfortunately *Henry V* has come to typify martial glory, success against fearsome odds, in a past we can feel is comfortably distant. Yes, the 'famous victory' is there, but so too is the contrasting mood of doubt and bitterness and an immediacy that can address us directly today.

REVISION QUESTIONS

1. 'The prologues are the first sign of Shakespeare's imperfect dramatic faith' (Mark Van Doren). Are they?

2. Consider the claim that *Henry V* should be considered an Epic. If it is an Epic, does that make it less a drama?

3. How would you defend *Henry V* from the charge that it is 'mere jingoism'?

4. What justification has a stage director for re-organising Shakespeare's text to create a new scene? (See 7.7)

5. How might an intelligently conceived production of *Henry V* strike (a) a French audience; (b) an American audience?

6. 'This play bears every mark of having been hastily written' (John Masefield). Consider the pros and cons of this remark.

7. Offer a counter-view to that given in Section 7, (a) to the way comedy is described; and (b) to its function. OR How is comedy used in *Henry V*?

8. Take up John Arden's suggestion that Shakespeare might have written 'a secret play within the official one' and apply it to your reading of *Henry V*. (See 7.9)

9. In what ways does a knowledge of history illuminate an understanding of *Henry V*?

10. '*Henry V* is as far as possible removed from what is generally

understood by drama' (Sidney Lee). Consider this assessment.

11. 'There is a seamy side to [Henry V's] wooing that cannot be so easily explained away' (Zdeněk Stříbrný). Can it be explained at all?

12. How does Shakespeare dramatise 'the victory of Agincourt'?

13. How different would *Henry V* be without the Prologue and Choruses?

APPENDIX:

SHAKESPEARE'S THEATRE

We should speak, as Muriel Bradbrook reminds us, not of the Elizabethan stage but of Elizabethan stages. Plays of Shakespeare were acted on tour, in the halls of mansions, one at least in Gray's Inn, frequently at Court and after 1609 at the Blackfriars, a small, roofed theatre for those who could afford the price. But even after his Company acquired the Blackfriars, we know of no play of his not acted (unless, rather improbably, *Troilus* is an exception) for the general public at the Globe, or before 1599 at its predecessor, the Theatre, which, since the Globe was constructed from the same timbers, must have resembled it. Describing the Globe, we can claim therefore to be describing, in an acceptable sense, Shakespeare's theatre, the physical structure his plays were designed to fit. Even in the few probably written for a first performance elsewhere, adaptability to that structure would be in his mind.

For the facilities of the Globe we have evidence from the drawing of the Swan theatre (based on a sketch made by a visitor to London about 1596) which depicts the interior of another public theatre; the builder's contract for the Fortune theatre, which in certain respects (fortunately including the dimensions and position of the stage) was to copy the Globe; indications in the dramatic texts; comments, like Ben Jonson's on the throne let down from above by machinery; and eye-witness testimony to the number of spectators (in round figures, 3000) accommodated in the auditorium.

In communicating with the audience, the actor was most favourably placed. Soliloquising at the centre of the front of the great platform, he was at the mid-point of the theatre, with no one among the spectators more than sixty feet away from him. That platform-stage (Figs I and II) was the most important feature for performance at the Globe. It has the audience – standing in the yard (10) and seated in the galleries (9) – on three sides of it. It was 43 feet wide, and $27^{1}/_{2}$ feet from front to back. Raised ($?5^{1}/_{2}$ feet) above the

SHAKESPEARE'S THEATRE

The stage and its adjuncts; the tiring-house; and the auditorium.

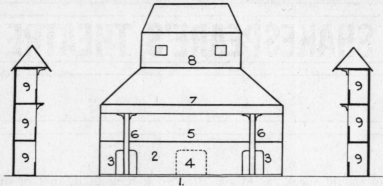

FIG I ELEVATION

1. Platform stage (approximately five feet above the ground) 2. Tiring-house
3. Tiring-house doors to stage 4. Conjectured third door 5. Tiring-house gallery (balustrade and partitioning not shown) 6. Pillars supporting the heavens 7. The heavens 8. The hut 9. The spectators' galleries

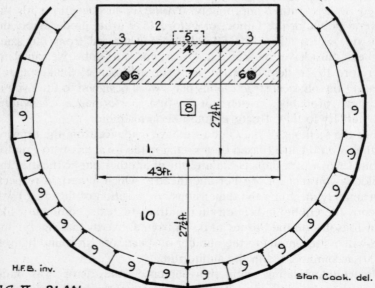

H.F.B. inv.

Stan Cook. del.

FIG II PLAN

1. Platform stage 2. Tiring-house 3. Tiring-house doors to stage
4. Conjectural third door 5. Conjectural discovery space (alternatively behind 3)
6. Pillars supporting the heavens 7. The heavens 8. Trap door 9. Spectators' gallery 10. The yard

The Globe

An Artist's imaginative recreation of a typical Elizabethan theatre.

level of the yard, it had a trap-door (II.8) giving access to the space below it. The actors, with their equipment, occupied the 'tiring house' (attiring-house: 2) immediately at the back of the stage. The stage-direction 'within' means inside the tiring-house. Along its frontage, probably from the top of the second storey, juts out the canopy or 'Heavens', carried on two large pillars rising through the platform (6,7) and sheltering the rear part of the stage, the rest of which, like the yard, was open to the sky. If the 'hut' (1.8), housing the machinery for descents, stood, as in the Swan drawing, above the 'Heavens', that covering must have had a trap-door, so that the descents could be made through it.

Descents are one illustration of the vertical dimension the dramatist could use to supplement the playing-area of the great platform. The other opportunities are provided by the tiring-house frontage or facade. About this facade the evidence is not as complete or clear as we should like, so that Fig. I is in part conjectural. Two doors giving entry to the platform there certainly were (3). A third (4) is probable but not certain. When curtained, a door, most probably this one, would furnish what must be termed a discovery-space (II.5), not an inner stage (on which action in any depth would have been out of sight for a significant part of the audience). Usually no more than two actors were revealed (exceptionally, three), who often then moved out on to the platform. An example of this is Ferdinand and Miranda in *The Tempest* 'discovered' at chess, then seen on the platform speaking with their fathers. Similarly the gallery (I.5) was not an upper stage. Its use was not limited to the actors: sometimes it functioned as 'lords' rooms' for favoured spectators, sometimes, perhaps, as a musicians' gallery. Frequently the whole gallery would not be needed for what took place aloft: a window-stage (as in the first balcony scene in *Romeo*, even perhaps in the second) would suffice. Most probably this would be a part (at one end) of the gallery itself; or just possibly, if the gallery did not (as it does in the Swan drawing) extend the whole width of the tiring-house, a window over the left or right-hand door. As the texts show, whatever was presented aloft, or in the discovery-space, was directly related to the action on the platform, so that at no time was there left, between the audience and the action of the drama, a great bare space of platform-stage. In relating Shakespeare's drama to the physical conditions of the theatre, the primacy of that platform is never to be forgotten.

Note: The present brief account owes most to C. Walter Hodges, *The Globe Restored*; Richard Hosley in *A New Companion to Shakespeare Studies*, and the *The Revels History of English Drama*; and to articles by Hosley and Richard Southern in *Shakespeare Survey*, 12, 1959, where full discussion can be found.

HAROLD BROOKS

FURTHER READING

Historical background
Alfred Hart, *Shakespeare and the Homilies* (Melbourne, 1934).
B. L. Joseph, *Shakespeare's Eden: The Commonwealth of England 1558–1629* (Blandford, 1971).
J. A. Mazzeo, *Renaissance and Revolution* (Secker & Warburg 1967).
Peter Saccio, *Shakespeare's English Kings* (New York: Oxford University Press 1977).

Elizabethan theatre
R. A. Foakes, *Illustrations of the English Stage 1580–1642* (Scolar, 1985).
Andrew Gurr, *The Shakespearean Stage 1574–1642* (Cambridge University Press, 1970).
Peter Thomson, *Shakespeare's Theatre* (Routledge & Kegan Paul, 1983).

Sources
G. Bullough, *Narrative and Dramatic Sources of Shakespeare*, *iv* (London, 1962).

Production history
Sally Beauman (ed.), *The RSC's Production of 'Henry V' for the Centenary Season at the Royal Shakespeare Theatre* (Pergamon, 1976).
Harry M. Geduld, *Filmguide to 'Henry V'* (Indiana University Press, 1973).
Arthur Colby Sprague, *Shakespeare's Histories: Plays for the Stage* (London, 1964).

General studies
Lilly B. Campbell, *Shakespeare's 'Histories': Mirrors of Elizabethan Policy* (San Marino, 1947).

E. A. M. Colman, *The Dramatic Use of Bawdy in Shakespeare* (Longman, 1974).

P. Davison, *Popular Appeal in English Drama to 1850* (Macmillan, 1982).

Essay collections

Michael Quinn (ed.) *Shakespeare*: 'Henry V' (Macmillan Casebook. 1969).

W. A. Armstrong (ed.) *Shakespeare's Histories: An Anthology of Modern Criticism* (Penguin, 1972).

E. M. Waith (ed.) *Shakespeare: The Histories* (Twentieth-Century Views, 1965).

Critical Studies of Henry V

Leonard F. Dean, 'From *Richard II* to *Henry V*: A Closer View', in *Twentieth-century Interpretations of* 'Richard II', (ed.) Paul M Cubeta (New Jersey, 1971).

Harley Granville-Barker, *From 'Henry V' to Hamlet,* in *Studies in Shakespeare* (ed.) P. Alexander (London, 1964).

Leslie Hotson, *Shakespeare's Sonnets Dated and Other Essays* (New York: Oxford University Press, 1949), for Pistol.

John Palmer, 'Henry of Monmouth' in *Political and Comic Characters of Shakespeare* (Macmillan, 1945).

A. P. Rossiter, 'Ambivalence: The Dialectic of Histories', in *Angel with Horns* (London, 1961).

E. E. Stoll, *Poets and Playwrights* (University of Minnesota, 1930) for Henry V essay.

Zdeněk Stříbrný, 'Henry V and History' in *Shakespeare in a Changing World*, ed. Arnold Kettle (London, 1964).

Charles Williams, 'Henry V' in *Shakespeare Criticism 1919–1935*, selected by Anne Ridler (Oxford University Press, 1936).